Ace Your Case® III: Practice Makes Perfect

2nd Edition

WetFeet, Inc.

The Folger Building

101 Howard Street

Suite 300

San Francisco, CA 94105

Phone: (415) 284-7900 or 1-800-926-4JOB

Fax: (415) 284-7910

Website: www.WetFeet.com

Ace Your Case® III: Practice Makes Perfect

ISBN: 1-58207-298-1

Table of Contents

Nailing the Case 53

Ace Your Case III at a Glance

Case-by-Case Rules

Here's a summary of the different types of cases you'll find in this report, along with some rules that should help you ace your answer.

Market-Sizing Questions

- Use round numbers
- Show your work
- Use paper and calculator

Business Operations Questions

- Isolate the main issue
- Apply a framework
- Think "action"

Business Strategy Questions

- Think "frameworks"
- Ask questions
- Work from big to small

Resume Cases

- Know your story
- Keep the Parent Test in mind
- Let your excitement shine

The Interview Unplugged

- Overview

- The Case Interview

Overview

When it comes to preparing for your case interviews, there's one word and one word only: practice. By now, you're spending all of your spare time thinking about why Dell is getting into printers, why the utility industry is consolidating, and how much mustard is consumed in Idaho. Your family thinks you're strange, but you're on the right track. By now, you're probably even starting to enjoy thinking about these issues. Watch out: You might be turning into a consultant.

This guide is designed to be a companion volume to *Ace Your Case* and *Ace Your Case II*. It offers more-detailed explanations about different case types and more sample questions. We've also incorporated information from you, our customers, about what you're hearing in the cubicle. Many of our sample case questions here are based on real, live case questions that people received in their interviews last year.

For those who haven't seen our other case-interviewing guides, *Ace Your Case* discusses the consulting interview in general and offers a primer containing a number of common frameworks and B-school–type tools (watch out for the 3Cs and the 4Ps, not to mention the infamous Five Forces) that should help you attack your case questions. *Ace Your Case II* contains 15 specific case questions and detailed recommended answers.

A word about how to use this guide: We strongly recommend that you try to solve the questions first, without looking at the answers. After you've given them your best shot, go ahead and check out our recommended answers. If you find that our "good answer" differs from yours, see if there's something you can learn from our suggestions. But don't panic—there are usually numerous ways to answer any case question. It's far more important to note the approach and the likely responses from the interviewer. As you sharpen those skills, keep thinking to yourself, "I love these case questions!" Pretty soon you'll find yourself talking like a consultant!

The Case Interview

Background

Many management consulting firms, especially the strategy firms (McKinsey, The Boston Consulting Group, Bain, Mercer, et al.) love to give prospective employees a problem to solve during the course of the interview. These problem-solving exercises, known generally as "case questions," are designed to help the interviewer screen candidates and determine which people really have what it takes to be a real, live, card-carrying management consultant.

Case questions come in many forms and levels of complexity. To help you get a handle on them, we have identified four different categories of questions:

1. Market-sizing questions

2. Business operations questions

3. Business strategy questions

4. Resume questions

Try to make the interview more of a dialogue between equals. Try to have fun.

(Note that we are not covering the brainteaser category in this Insider Guide. Consulting firms rarely ask brainteaser questions; other types of cases give much more insight into the type of thinking that makes a good consultant.)

Each of these prototypes has certain distinguishing features, which we discuss below. In addition, our insiders recommend certain "rules of the road" that should help you successfully navigate the different types of questions. Don't worry—you'll never be asked to spit out a category name and serial number for the questions you receive in the interview cubicle. Nevertheless, if you can identify the type of question, you will have a better idea about how to effectively attack the problem.

What Your Interviewer Is Seeking

It may seem as if your interviewer is using the case technique for one purpose alone: to humiliate prospective consultants. Although a few interviewers do seem to take a perverse pleasure in watching candidates writhe, this isn't the top goal of the technique. According to insiders, case questions really do help them evaluate a candidate's aptitude for consulting. What does that mean exactly? Whether you're an undergrad, an MBA, or a PhD, consulting interviewers will likely depend on the case questions to check you out on the following dimensions:

- Analytical ability
- Intelligence
- Ability to not break into hives under pressure
- Common sense
- Ability to think on your feet
- Interest in problem solving

- Business intuition

- Facility with numbers

- Presentation skills

- Communication skills

- Ability to sort through information and focus on the key points

- Ability to analyze and then make recommendations based on the analysis

- Creativity

- Enthusiasm

Before you bid all your points to get an interview with name-your-consulting-firm, we recommend that you spend some time thinking about how consulting fits you. In particular, you must have good answers to two questions: Why do you want to be a consultant? And, why do you want to work for this firm?

If you have good answers to these two questions, then you're ready to start thinking about cases. We start by discussing the case interview as it relates to several categories of candidates: undergraduates, MBAs, advanced-degree candidates, and experienced hires.

Undergraduates

Consulting interviewers tell us that the case questions and the expected answers for undergraduates tend to be simpler and more understandable than those for MBA students. Market-sizing questions are very popular (you will almost certainly get at least one of these), as are general business strategy problems. In the business strategy area, the companies and the topics may also seem a little more friendly; you're more likely to get a case about a beer company than about a company trying to license the latest packet-filtering technology for data encryption. Operations questions (with the exception of the ever-popular declining-profits question) are less common for undergraduates, and resume questions will more likely focus on academic or extracurricular activities than on work experiences.

Interviewers tell us that they often provide more prompting to undergraduate candidates during the interview. In evaluating your answer to a question, only the most sadistic interviewer would expect you to regurgitate all the standard business-school terminology and techniques (after all, how else could the company justify paying MBAs the big bucks?). But beware: Rank amateurs are definitely not welcome. Thus, you must have a general understanding of basic business relationships (e.g., revenues – costs = profits), but don't get your knickers in a knot if you can't name even one of the Five Forces.

Here are a few real, live case questions fielded by our undergraduate customers:

- Your client, a tire manufacturer, is evaluating entry into a new market: the market for four-wheel-drive-vehicle tires. How do you estimate the size of the market?

- What's the weight of the Statue of Liberty?

- If a publishing company wanted to start a new interior decorating magazine, what would it have to think about?

- If you're working for General Mills, and Kellogg's introduces a frequent-buyer program, should you follow suit?

MBAs

MBAs have long been the heavy hitters of the consulting workforce. As a result, the case interview reaches its most sophisticated and demanding form in the MBA interview. All types of questions—from the simple market-sizer to the gnarliest of business strategy problems—are fair game. Practically any industry or functional issue area is possible material for the case question. An MBA candidate will be expected to be familiar with a number of the standard MBA frameworks and concepts. Also, the case will possibly have a few tricky twists or turns. For example, what might seem like a pure and simple international strategy question might be complicated by an unexpected restriction related to the European regulatory environment.

Interviewers tell us that most MBAs have a polished interview technique and understand the basics of many case problems. Therefore, they look for depth in the answer (what they describe as an ability to get several levels down in the answer) and a real familiarity with business concepts. We understand that at least some recruiters like to ask resume case questions because they provide an opportunity to get more detail about the candidate's background and problem-solving experiences.

Here are a few real, live case questions fielded by our MBA customers:

- How many AA batteries are sold in Montana in a year?

- A bank wants to reduce costs and asks you for advice about closing a specific branch. What should you consider?

- A wealthy entrepreneur has just bought a baseball team, and he asks you for advice on how to show increased profits in a year. What do you suggest?

- A pharmaceutical company is considering changing its sales strategy from using a sales force with geographic territories to using specific locations. What financial analysis would you use to see if this is worthwhile?

Advanced-Degree Candidates (Non-MBAs)

Although consulting firms are attracting record numbers of MBA applicants, several of the top firms have started to look beyond traditional feeder programs to identify top talent. According to WetFeet customers and recruiters, the different firms have very different approaches to advanced degree candidates. McKinsey and BCG, among others, have launched aggressive recruiting programs aimed at PhDs, MDs, JDs, and others at the top schools. In the process, some of these firms have created customized recruiting and training programs for advanced-degree candidates. Other firms continue to consider advanced-degree candidates on a case-by-case basis, often pitting them against undergraduate or MBA candidates, depending on their background.

Whether or not you enter a separate recruiting track, we understand from our customers that the format for the interviews is similar to that of undergraduate and MBA recruiting programs. In other words, expect a heavy dose of case interview questions along with the general get-to-know-you queries. One slight difference is that, in addition to seeing whether or not you can handle the substance of the case question, the recruiter will also be looking to see "if [you] can break out of the PhD box." In other words, can you adapt to the real world and answer questions without giving too much detail?

According to WetFeet customers, case questions for advanced-degree candidates usually don't require you to carry your own MBA toolbox. Instead, the questions may relate to previous research (your resume is usually a font of material), or they may resemble undergraduate case studies that check a person's intuition, common sense, analytical skills, and problem-solving abilities. According to interviewers at the firms, they may be more inclined to prompt candidates with questions, and they may be satisfied with a good, solid analytical answer that doesn't necessarily incorporate all the latest business buzzwords.

Check out these case questions fielded by our advanced-degree customers:

- How many windows are there in Mexico City?
- Question for someone who had majored in international relations: Why have missiles with MIRVed warheads caused the most trouble in arms-control discussions?
- An automobile insurance company has asked you to tell it why it has been experiencing a decline in profits.
- American Express has hired you to help it increase the profitability of the Amex Green Card. What do you advise doing?

Experienced Hires

If you are seeking to join a consulting firm from industry, or from another consulting firm, your interviewing experience may differ from that described in this report. According to WetFeet customers, experienced-hire candidates may or may not face a battery of case questions. There is no hard-and-fast rule, but it seems as though people with more experience (10-plus years), and people who have already worked for a name-brand consulting firm, are relatively unlikely to face a case as part of their review process. In contrast, people who have worked in industry for a few years and who are seeking to enter at a middle level are likely to go through a process similar to that used for MBAs (i.e., expect lots of cases). In particular, if you are changing careers (e.g., moving from nonprofit work to consulting) and not signing on as an industry authority, you'll probably be scrutinized for your consulting aptitude—as demonstrated by your ability to field case questions.

Typical case questions faced by our experienced-hire customers include:

- Your client is a struggling telecom firm. How would you turn it around?

- Your client is a U.S.-based company that sells telephones by mail. Mail sales of telephones are a small portion of the company's overall business, and sales are below average for mail-order sales of appliances. Should the client continue to sell phones in this way? If so, how should it make the operation more profitable?

- Specific questions related to their area of expertise.

Company-Specific Variations

As you enter the ring with consultants from a variety of firms, you'll probably notice differences in the questions you receive, as well as the style and approach of the case interview. More often than not, these differences derive from the differences in the personalities and experiences of your interviewers. However, several firms have developed their own approach to the case interview. One variation involves giving a candidate a written case prior to the interview and asking him or her to prepare to discuss the case in detail during the interview. We understand that PricewaterhouseCoopers has given preprinted cases to candidates the night before an interview. Monitor Company has used a similar technique in which the candidate will be given materials before the interview. Monitor has also used a group interview technique that requires competing candidates to work with each other to solve a problem.

One other thing to keep in mind: Recruiters suggest that you would be wise to keep the firm's reputation and areas of strength in mind as you launch into your case answer. Firms that are known for a particular type of work are likely to be more sensitive to those issues in the case questions they give. For example, if you're interviewing with Towers Perrin, you shouldn't be surprised to find a "people issue" somewhere in the case. If you're talking with Deloitte Consulting, keep "operations" in mind as you craft an answer—and don't talk about how it's important to work only with the company's top management. And, if you're interviewing with Bain, remember how much importance the company attaches to "measurable results" and "data-driven" analysis.

Case-by-Case Rules

- Market-Sizing Cases

- Business Operations Cases

- Business Strategy Cases

- Resume Cases

Market-Sizing Cases

Case-by-Case Rules

Overview

Consultants love to ask market-sizing questions. Not only are they easy to create, discuss, and evaluate, they are also highly representative of an important type of work done by consultants. In their simplest form, market-sizing cases require the candidate to determine the size of a particular market (hence the name). In the real world, this information can be especially helpful when gauging the attractiveness of a new market. In the interview context, a market-sizing question might be pitched in an extremely straightforward format (e.g., "What is the market for surfboards in the United States?"). Or it may be disguised as a more complex question (e.g., "Do you think Fidelity should come out with a mutual fund targeted at high-net-worth individuals?") which requires the respondent to peel away the extraneous detail in order to identify the market-sizing issue at the core. In a more highly developed variation, the interviewer might ask a strategy or operations case question that requires the respondent to do some market-sizing in order to come up with an appropriate recommendation.

The Scorecard

Market-sizing questions allow the interviewer to test the candidate's facility with numbers, powers of analysis, and common sense. For example, if you were asked to size the surfboard market, you would need to make basic assumptions about the market. (How many people surf? How many boards does a typical surfer dude own? How often will he or she get a new one? Are there other big purchasers besides individual surfers? Is there a market for used boards?) You would also need to make a few basic calculations (number of surfers X number of new boards per year + total quantity purchased by other types of customers, etc.). As you work through these issues, the interviewer would also get a glimpse of your common sense. (Did you assume that everybody in the U.S. population would be a potential surfer, or did you try to estimate the population in prime surfing areas like California and Hawaii?)

Location

Market-sizing questions can pop up in all interviews. They are almost certain to make an appearance in undergraduate and advanced-degree interviews. Indeed, WetFeet customers with BAs and PhDs report receiving exactly the same market-sizing questions. MBAs are also likely to receive market-sizing questions; however, a common and more complex variation typical of an MBA interview involves assessing the opportunity for a new product. For example, you might be asked whether your pharmaceutical company client should develop and market a drug for male pattern baldness. Part of the analysis would require you to estimate the market potential (i.e., market size) for the drug.

Manhandling Your Market-Sizing

Market-sizing questions can seem intimidating. But once you understand the rules (and practice your technique), you can come to view these cases as slow pitches right over the center of the plate. So, just how many golf balls are used in the United States in a year? You don't know, and the truth is, neither does your interviewer. In fact, your interviewer doesn't even care what the real number is. But remember, she does care about your ability to use logic, common sense, and creativity to get to a plausible answer. And she wants to make sure you don't turn tail when you've got a few numbers to run. Which brings us to the Rules for Market Sizing Questions.

Rule 1: Use round numbers. Even if you weren't a multivariate calculus stud, you can impress your interviewer with your number-crunching abilities if you stick to round numbers. They're much easier to add, subtract, multiply and divide, and since we've already decided that the exact answer doesn't matter anyway, go ahead and pick something that you can toss around with ease. Good examples? One hundred, one million, ten dollars, two, one-half. The population of the United States? Two-hundred-fifty million, give or take.

Rule 2: Show your work. Case questions are the ultimate "show your work" questions. In fact, your exact answer matters less than the path that took you there. Remember, the market-sizing question is merely a platform through which your interviewer can test your analysis, creativity, and comfort with numbers.

Rule 3: Write it down. If you feel more comfortable writing everything down and using a calculator, do! Most interviewers will not care if you use a pencil and paper to keep your thoughts organized and logical. And if pulling out the HP to multiply a few numbers keeps you from wigging out, then by all means do it. Your interviewer will be more impressed if you are cool, calm, and collected, and if using props helps you, then go for it.

Business Operations Cases

Overview

A fair number of case questions cover operations issues. Given the existing economic environment, in fact, the mix of consulting business has shifted more towards operations and process focused cases, so be prepared for a business operations case. Broadly speaking, "operations" refers to all the things involved in running a business and getting product out the door. In a manufacturing plant, this would include the purchasing and transporting of raw materials, the manufacturing processes, the scheduling of staff and facilities, the distribution of the product, the servicing of equipment in the field, and so on. In its broadest sense, operations would even include the sales and marketing of the company's products and the systems used to track sales. Where strategy questions deal with the future direction of the firm (such as whether to enter a new line of business), operations deals with the day-to-day running of the business. It is a particularly fertile ground for consulting work, and for case questions. Some of the most typical case questions of this type are those that require the candidate to explain why a company's sales or profits have declined.

The Scorecard

Consultants like to ask operations questions because they allow the interviewer to see whether the candidate understands fundamental issues related to running a business (e.g., the relationship between revenues and costs, and the relationship and impact of fixed costs and variable costs on a company's profitability). In addition, operations questions require the candidate to demonstrate a good grasp of process and an ability to sort through a pile of information and home in on the most important factors.

Location

Operations questions are fair game for all candidates, including undergraduates and advanced-degree candidates. According to our customers, the "declining profits" questions are some of the most popular types of cases around, and almost all candidates can expect to get several of these. That said, MBAs are typically expected to explore these questions in greater detail and have a better grasp of key business issues and terminology. MBAs could also get tossed more-complicated operations questions. For example, an MBA case might involve understanding the implications of allocating fixed costs in a certain way, or, perhaps, the impact on the balance sheet of a certain type of financing. Undergraduates and non-MBA candidates still need to be familiar with a few basic operational concepts, such as the relationship between costs and revenues, and the various things that might have an impact on them. In addition, under-graduates might expect that the topic of the question be more familiar. For example, an undergraduate might be asked about the implications of launching a new national chain of restaurants. An MBA might be asked about factors that would allow a manufacturing operation to increase throughput.

Optimizing Your Business Operations Answers

Operations case questions are more complex than market-sizing questions. Not only do they typically require basic business knowledge (or, in place of that, a good deal of common sense), but they also frequently require the candidate to think like a detective. For example, the interviewer might ask why an airline has been losing money while its market share has increased. There could be many reasons for this: Revenues might be down (and that, in turn, might be caused by any number of things, including ticket price wars, lower ridership, growing accounts payable, etc.), costs might be higher (due to higher fuel costs, greater landing fees, higher plane maintenance costs, etc.), or the airline could be operating more inefficiently (e.g., higher passenger loads might require it to lease additional aircraft or pay staff overtime). In any case, a successful analysis of the question requires the candidate to think clearly and efficiently about the question. To help with these types of questions, here are a couple of rules you might want to keep in mind:

Rule No. 1: Isolate the main issue! Operations questions usually have lots of potential answers. The first step in identifying a good answer (and demonstrating your analytical firepower) is to separate the wheat from the chaff. Once you have zeroed in on the main issue, you'll be able to apply your energy to working out a good conclusion to the problem.

Rule 2: Apply a framework! Frameworks were made for cracking operations questions! They will help you sift through lots of data and organize your answer. A useful framework can be something as simple as saying, "If the airline is losing money, it has something to do with either costs or revenues," and moving on to talk about each of these areas in turn.

Rule 3: Think action! Unlike your market-sizing question or brainteaser, operations questions never end with a nice, neat analysis. Rather, the goal here is action. The hypothetical client is usually facing a critical issue: Revenues are falling, costs are rising, production is crashing. Something needs to be done. As a consultant, you will be hired to give advice. As a candidate, you should be sensitive to the fact that your analysis must drive toward a solution. Even if you need more data before you're able to make a final recommendation, you should acknowledge that you are evaluating various courses of action. Better yet, you should lay out a plan for next steps.

Business Strategy Cases

Overview

Business-strategy cases are the granddaddies, and demons, of the case-question world. Consultants love to use these questions because they touch on so many different issues. A good strategy question can have a market-sizing piece, a logic puzzle, multiple operations issues, and a major dose of creativity and action thrown in for good measure. Moreover, a complex strategy question can go in many different directions, thereby allowing the interviewer to probe the candidate's abilities in a variety of areas. Again, strategy-case questions can run the gamut from complex, multi-industry, multi-national, multi-issue behemoths to a localized question with a pinpoint focus. Common types of strategy questions include advising a client about an acquisition, responding to a competitive move by another company in the industry, and evaluating opportunities for a new product introduction and pricing the product.

The Scorecard

Depending on the nature of the question, the interviewer can use it to assess anything and everything from your ability to handle numbers to your ability to wade through a mass of detailed information and synthesize it into a compelling business strategy. Of all the different types of case questions, these are also the most like the actual work you'll do on the job (at least at the strategy firms). One other thing the interviewer will be checking carefully: your presentation abilities.

Location

Strategy-case questions are fair game for any type of candidate. For under-graduates, they will often be more two-dimensional and straightforward. For MBA candidates, they will frequently have several layers of issues, and perhaps an international or other twist to boot. Although most strategy boutiques will use this kind of case as a mainstay in their recruiting efforts, firms with more of an operations focus may rely more heavily on operations questions.

Succeeding at the Strategy Stumpers

Because business strategy questions can involve many different elements, they can inspire fear in the weak of heart. Although it is true that strategy questions can be the most difficult, they can also be the most fun. This is your oppor-tunity to play CEO, or at least advisor to the CEO. You can put all of your business intuition and your hard-nosed, data-driven research to work and come up with a plan that will bring a huge multi-national corporation into the limelight—or not. Does it matter that you just crafted a story about why a credit-card company should go into the Italian market when your best friend who interviewed immediately prior to you recommended against going Italian? No, not really. Unless, of course, your friend did a better job of exploring the case question. What does that mean? By going through this case book (and the other WetFeet Ace Your Case! Insider Guides), you're already a step ahead of the game. However, here are a couple of rules you'll want to keep in mind as you tackle your strategy-case questions.

Rule 1: Think frameworks! While analyzing a really juicy strategy question you might be able to draw information and jargon out of almost every course in your school's core business curriculum. Don't succumb to temptation! Your interviewer will be much more impressed by a clear and simple story about how you are attacking the question and where you are going with your analysis. The best way to do this is to apply a framework to the problem. Just as with operations questions, this means setting out a plan of attack up front and following it through to conclusion. One other big benefit: Having a clear framework will help you organize your analysis.

Rule 2: Ask questions. Successful consulting is as much about asking the right question as it is about providing a good answer. Likewise, your solution to a strategy case will be much better if you've focused your energy on the right issue. To help you get there, don't hesitate to ask your interviewer questions. In the best case, he may help you avoid a derailment; in the worst case, he'll understand your thought process as you plow through the analysis.

Rule 3: Work from big to small. Even though the strategy case you are examining was the subject of a study that lasted several months, you probably have about 15 minutes to provide your answer. Therefore, it's essential that you start by looking at the most significant issues first. Besides, this is a great discipline for future consultants. After all, the client will probably be paying for your time by the hour, so you'll want to make sure that you are really adding value.

Resume Cases

Overview

One favorite type of alternative case question is the resume case. Instead of cooking up a case question based on a carefully disguised project from his files, the interviewer will pull something straight from the candidate's resume. Usually, these cases stem from a previous professional experience, but occasionally you'll get something like: "I see you play rugby. Describe for me all the different positions on a rugby team, and the play strategy for each." Frequently, the interviewer will ask the candidate to walk through a previous work project or experience and explain how he or she decided on a particular course of action. As the candidate goes through the discussion, the interviewer may then change a few critical assumptions and ask the candidate to explain how he or she would have responded. For example, if you had started and run a successful computer repair service, the interviewer might ask how you would have responded had a local computer store created a knock-off service and offered it at a lower price.

The Scorecard

The resume case is a way for the interviewer to dig a little deeper into your resume and at the same time test your case-cracking capabilities. (It also provides a little variety throughout a grueling day of interviews.) Here, the interviewer is testing for your ability to communicate—in layman's terms—a topic that is very familiar to you. Resume cases are generally a good opportunity for you to toot your own horn a bit about your past experience and exude confidence, competence, and enthusiasm about things you really understand.

Location

The resume question is fair game for undergrads, MBAs, and advanced-degree candidates. Naturally, because the resumes for each type of candidate differ significantly, the types of questions also differ. MBAs can expect business-oriented questions; advanced-degree candidates can expect questions related to their previous research. We understand that resume cases are a particularly popular type of question for PhD students. Not only do they allow the candidate to avoid feeling like he or she has to master a whole new lexicon and body of frameworks, they test his or her communications skills.

Rocking Your Resume Case

Because the resume-case question takes the discussion to your home turf, there isn't really a secret recipe for pulling apart the question. Rather, the way to be successful here is to follow a few basic interview rules.

Rule 1: Know your story. Nothing will make you look worse—and help you find the door more quickly—than not knowing what you put on your own resume. Make sure you have reviewed all of the items on your resume before the interview. Write down a few notes about what you did at each job, and the main message you want to convey through each bullet point on your resume. Think up a short story for each bullet point that will provide compelling evidence to support those messages.

Rule 2: The Parent Test. This is not the place to play the polyglot; nobody will be impressed with your ability to speak techno-babble. The interviewer will assume that you know everything there is to know about your area of expertise, whether that's molecular biology or your computer-repair service. The real question is: Can you tell others about what you did without sending them into a coma? It may sound easy, but many people seem incapable of communicating what they know. Our suggestion? Practice talking about your work as if you were telling your parents.

Rule 3: Let your excitement shine! This is your home field, so use it to your advantage. Talk about your past work with energy and enthusiasm. Believe it or not, even consultants like a little passion. Besides, if you're sitting there griping about a previous work experience, guess what's running through your interviewer's mind: "Whoa, Nelly. This cat could be trouble!"

The Practice Range

- Market-Sizing Questions

- Business Operations Questions

- Business Strategy Questions

- Resume Questions

Market-Sizing Questions

Remember the rules for market-sizing questions:

1. Use round numbers.

2. Show your work.

3. Write it down.

How many pieces of candy are given out on Halloween each year in the United States?

Key questions to ask:

_____

_____

_____

_____

Basic equations/numbers:

_____

_____

_____

_____

How you'd track the numbers down:

_____

_____

_____

_____

_____

Case 2

What is the average number of chairs in a house?

Key questions to ask:

_____

_____

_____

_____

Basic equations/numbers:

_____

_____

_____

_____

How you'd track the numbers down:

_____

_____

_____

_____

Case 3

How many blue jeans are sold in the United States each year?

Key questions to ask:

Basic equations/numbers:

How you'd track the numbers down:

Case 4

How many unique people attend events at the Rose Bowl every year?

Key questions to ask:

_____

_____

_____

_____

Basic equations/numbers:

_____

_____

_____

_____

How you'd track the numbers down:

_____

_____

_____

_____

Business Operations Questions

Remember the rules for business operations questions:

1. Isolate the main issue.

2. Apply a framework.

3. Think action.

Case 5

A leading breakfast cereal manufacturer has hired you to determine why its profits have taken a dive in the last year. What should it do to improve its performance?

Key questions to ask:

_____

_____

_____

_____

_____

_____

What are the main issues?

_____

_____

_____

_____

_____

_____

_____

Case 5 (continued)

Key approaches/frameworks:

Possible courses of action:

A regional bank interested in expanding beyond commercial banking services has merged with a major asset-management firm. They are struggling with post-merger integration and have hired you to help them. What issues would you address?

Key questions to ask:

What are the main issues?

Key approaches/frameworks:

Possible courses of action:

Case 7

The owner of a hip college hangout called "Beer, Spaghetti and Exotic Desserts" recently hired a new manager and bartender to address a slump in customer volume. Customer volume quickly turned around, but the owner has noticed that profits have dropped. What is wrong?

Key questions to ask:

What process would you use to investigate this question?

Where would you find the information you need?

Case 8

The Director of Purchasing for the aircraft maintenance division of a major airline has asked for your help. His supplier base has grown to more than 500 vendors, who supply approximately 100,000 different aircraft parts to the airline. He has realized that his supplier strategy is suboptimal, both from a cost and efficiency standpoint. How would you help him devise a supplier strategy?

Key questions to ask:

What are the main issues?

Case 8 (continued)

Key approaches/frameworks:

_____

_____

_____

_____

_____

Possible courses of action:

_____

_____

_____

_____

_____

Action recommendations:

_____

_____

_____

_____

Business Strategy Questions

Keep the rules for business strategy questions in mind:

1. Think framework.

2. Ask questions.

3. Work from small to big.

Case 9

A small manufacturer and distributor of women's surf clothes is considering selling to high-end boutiques and has hired you to help out. What kinds of issues would you think about to help it make the decision?

Key questions to ask:

_____

_____

_____

_____

_____

What are the main issues?

_____

_____

_____

_____

_____

_____

Key approaches/frameworks:

_____

_____

_____

_____

Outline for my answer:

_____

_____

_____

_____

Action recommendations:

_____

_____

_____

_____

Your client is a large owner and operator of hotels and vacation properties. It also runs a highly successful rewards program that gives guests the opportunity to earn points for each stay. The company is considering partnering with small bed-and-breakfasts and offering guests the opportunity to earn points for stays at participating B&Bs as well. Should it go ahead with this partnership? What should it think about in order to make its decision?

Key questions to ask:

What are the main issues?

Key approaches/frameworks:

_____

_____

_____

_____

Outline for my answer:

_____

_____

_____

_____

Action recommendations:

_____

_____

_____

_____

Case 11

A camera company has stumbled on a compound that helps extend the life of cut roses. It wants to know if it should introduce the product and how to price it. The firm has collected the following data and wants your assistance in analyzing the data and making a recommendation:

- One billion roses are purchased each year in the United States.
- The average rose costs $2.
- There are 50 million unique buyers of roses.
- The chemical extends the life of cut roses by one week.
- There are five other products on the market that extend the life of cut roses from two to five days.
- Five grams per rose of the new chemical must be present in order to be effective.
- It costs $0.02 per gram to manufacture the new chemical, including fixed and variable costs.

Key questions to ask:

_____

_____

_____

_____

What are the main issues?

_____

_____

_____

Key approaches/frameworks:

Outline for my answer:

Action recommendations:

Case 12

Your client is a large private equity firm. It is looking into "rolling up" the tow-truck industry; that is, buying many small- and medium-sized firms and combining them to create one, larger firm. It wants your help in assessing industry attractiveness.

Key questions to ask:

What are the main issues?

Outline for my answer:

Resume Questions

Remember the rules for resume questions:

1. Know your story

2. The Parent Test

3. Let your excitement shine

Case 13

After one year with our firm, what would our formal evaluation of your performance look like?

Case 14

I see that you worked at a dot com for a year, before moving to a large bank for two years. What do you see as the pros and cons for you of working in a large organization vs. a small organization? What would you bring to consulting from your experiences in two very different working environments?

I see you led a cross-functional merger integration team at General
Electric. What is your leadership style?

Nailing the Case

- Marketing-Sizing Questions

- Business Operations Questions

- Business Strategy Questions

- Resume Questions

Now it's time to walk through several answers to each of the questions given in the previous section. Although we believe that our recommended answers are good, we know that there are many other even better answers out there. Remember, though, the destination is often less important to your interviewer than the road you take to get there. With that in mind, smooth sailing! A quick note on the layout: Each question is followed by bad answers and a good answer. The questions and dialogue between the hypothetical recruiter and candidate appear in normal type; the WetFeet analysis and commentary appear in italics.

Market-Sizing Questions

Case 1

How many pieces of candy are given out on Halloween each year in the United States?

This is a straightforward market-sizing question, which would be good for undergraduates and advanced-degree candidates. It requires no special technical knowledge, and it focuses on a subject that is accessible—and hopefully enjoyed!—by everyone: Halloween candy.

Bad Answers

- 10 million.

  It's never good to just give a specific number answer, even if you happen to know the right number. This is especially true if the question asks you to estimate the market size of a product or industry in which you may have some experience, though hopefully the interviewer would be smart enough not to ask you such a question.

Rather, the interviewer is trying to see how you go about figuring out such an answer. After all, throughout your career as a consultant, you'll rarely find that you already know a needed number, and even if you do, you'll still have to show the client how you got the information.

- I never went trick-or-treating because I don't like candy.
  Though your aversion to sweets may be admirable, you're going to have to answer the question anyway.

- I always got the most candy because I made my own costumes.
  Bye bye.

- What does Halloween candy have to do with consulting?
  Good question, bad answer.

Good Answer

Candidate: Interesting question. It appears to me that there are two ways of attacking this problem. The first way is to determine how many people go trick-or-treating and multiply that number by the average number of pieces of candy they collect on their rounds. This would estimate "demand." The other way to answer the question is to estimate the "supply" side by determining how many houses give out candy every year, and multiplying that number by the number of pieces of candy each house distributes. Hopefully these two numbers will be about the same. Given our time constraints and the fact that I am more familiar with how many pieces of candy someone receives, I'd like to estimate the demand side.

The candidate has done a great job of providing an analytical framework of how she will attack the problem and outlined a couple of options for coming up with the answer. Further, the candidate has made a decision based on her experience: she is going to estimate the demand side. At this point, it's okay for the candidate to put the supply side question aside because the interviewer knows that she's acknowledged it; if the candidate had more time, she could do both. Nice start so far.

Candidate: Now, how many people go out trick-or-treating each year? First, let's figure out who is going trick-or-treating. Let's assume that you start trick-or-treating once you're five and you stop when you're 12. So our "market" is five to 12 year olds. Further, let's assume that the population of the United States is 250 million; what we need to estimate now is, of that 250 million, how many are five to 12 year olds. For the sake of argument, let's say that 25 million are in that age range—10 percent of the population. The way I got to this number was to assume that the average life expectancy is around 80, I'm looking at a seven-year age range, and there are more people at the lower end of the age spectrum than the higher end. Now what we need to do is determine what percentage of this 25 million goes out trick-or-treating on Halloween. I grew up in a neighborhood where almost everyone went trick-or-treating— maybe 75 percent of kids—but that seems really high to me, so let's say that 60 percent of kids in that age range collect candy each year. Conveniently, it also makes the math work. So there are 15 million kids who go out trick-or-treating.

Note what the candidate is doing. She is very logically breaking the problem down in pieces, narrowing the size of the market down. She is announcing assumptions to the interviewer, using round numbers, and basing her assumptions on previous experience. Remember: the accuracy of the assumptions is not as important as the analytic path the candidate takes to make them. And don't get caught up in the details—notice how the interviewer didn't try to disaggregate the percent of kids who go out trick-or-treating; the candidate may want to mention that it may differ by geography or location (urban vs. suburban vs. rural), but should leave it at that.

Candidate: So I have one of the key pieces of my equation; now I need to estimate how many pieces of candy each kid gets. The way I'm going to take a crack at this is to multiply the number of houses that each kid goes to by the average number of pieces of candy received per house.

Consultants are simple-minded people: keep the interviewer informed of where you've been and where you're going!

Candidate: When I went trick-or-treating, I probably went to 20 houses. The number of pieces of candy that I'd get from each house varied—for example, sometimes people would give out a large candy bar, others would give out lots of little pieces of candy. I'd say on average, I'd receive about five pieces of candy per house—again, this number will vary based on geography and location, but let's assume five pieces per house and 20 houses. Again, this makes the math easy: 100 pieces of candy per kid. Although I must admit when I think about dumping out my bag at the end of the night, 100 pieces seems high to me. But for now let's use that number. So 15 million kids times 100 pieces of candy is 1.5 billion pieces of candy. The way I would check this is to analyze the "supply" side and see if the numbers were close.

Note how the candidate is sanity checking her work and noting the places where numbers could be high or low and offering up a solution for checking the final result.

Case 2

What is the average number of chairs in a house?

This is a deceptively tricky question: though it centers around a topic accessible to everyone, it can get very detailed very quickly. Be careful in questions such as these that you continue to see the forest for the trees.

Bad Answers

- I haven't lived in a house for a while, but I can tell you how many chairs are in the average apartment.

  Again, you're going to have to answer the question that was asked of you. Remember that it's not the accuracy of the final answer, but rather the logic and structure of the thought process that got you there.

- I'd say about 20.

  Where'd this come from? How did you get there? Telling a consultant an answer without explaining how you got there is one way to bomb an interview.

Good Answer

Candidate: Well, I've never really thought about this, but let's take a crack at it. Here are a couple of things that come to mind. First of all, there are lots of different types of chairs. I'm going to assume that when you say chairs, you mean all kinds of chairs—dining room chairs, desk chairs, living room chairs, patio chairs, etc. Secondly, there are lots of different types of houses—small, medium, large—each with a different number of chairs. I'm also going to assume that we're excluding apartments, condos, and other types of residences in the analysis. So, to answer this question, I'm going to have to take the weighted average of the number of chairs in each house size.

This is a great start. The candidate has given an excellent overview of the problem; this establishes a lot of credibility with the interviewer. Additionally, the candidate has demonstrated an understanding of weighted averages, an oft-used analysis in consulting. When possible, try to show the interviewer early that you have cracked the case early by providing an analytic framework. Also, note how the candidate has narrowed the scope by making some reasonable and simplifying assumptions.

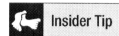

Candidate: First, let's talk about the different types of houses. For simplicity sake, I'm going to assume that there are three "buckets" of housing—small, medium, and large. Most of the houses are going to fall into the medium category, and there are likely more small houses than large ones. So I'm going to say that 50 percent of houses fall into the "medium" category, 30 percent fall into the small category, and 20 percent fall into the large category. Now what I need to do is figure out how many chairs there are in each type of home. Let's start out by figuring out how many chairs are in a small house, and then move up progressively to estimate how many chairs are in the medium and large houses.

Again, the candidate has done a good job of keeping the interviewer informed of where he is going and making key assumptions along the way. Establishing three buckets of houses is reasonable—avoid making the problem more complicated, particularly since it appears that this case is going to require you to keep track of quite a few numbers. Also, building up the number of chairs from small house to large house allows the candidate to build upon earlier assumptions.

Candidate: So, small houses probably have two bedrooms, two bathrooms, a living room, dining room, a kitchen, and probably one other room and small front and back yards. Of those rooms, the bedrooms and bathrooms probably won't have any chairs, so we can forget about those rooms for the time being. Now, let's make assumptions for the following rooms: the living room will probably have one large chair, the dining room will probably have room for four chairs, the "other" room might have one desk chair, and let's assume that the back yard has a small outdoor table with four more chairs. So this is an average of 10 chairs in the small house category.

The average medium house will probably have an extra bedroom, maybe another bathroom, and larger dining rooms, living rooms, and outdoor space. Again, let's assume that the bedroom and bathrooms have no chairs, so there is no difference there. There are probably six chairs at the dining room table and likely one additional chair in the living room, so that's an additional two indoor chairs. For the sake of argument, let's assume that there are an extra two outdoor chairs in a medium house. So that's a total of four extra chairs, or 14 chairs.

The candidate is progressing logically. Remember that the accuracy of the assumptions is not as critical as the logical path.

Candidate: The same analytic framework will apply to large houses. Large houses will have more bedrooms and bathrooms, and larger living rooms, dining rooms, and outdoor space. Let's assume that the same increase in the number of chairs exists—that there are four more chairs in these rooms. However, these houses may also have additional rooms, such as a den. Let's assume that there are three chairs in this room. This means that large houses have seven more chairs than medium houses, or 21 chairs. Therefore, the weighted average will be:

$$(10 \times 0.3) + (14 \times 0.5) + (21 \times 0.2) = 3 + 7 + 4.2 = 14.2 \text{ chairs}$$

Make sure that you've written your estimates down as you go, and write down the equation. Take your time figuring out the numbers. The interviewer would much rather wait while you do the math than have you be sloppy with the numbers.

Case 3

How many blue jeans are sold in the United States each year?

This is a straightforward question and there are several ways of answering it.

Bad Answers

- I used to work for a retail company, so I have a pretty good sense of how many jeans are sold.

  As previously mentioned, the interviewer is not seeking a specific answer; rather, he or she is looking for how you think and make assumptions. You should use prior—and relevant—experience only for making logical assumptions and testing your final answer.

- I don't really know anything about the jeans market.

  As a future consultant, you will often work in industries where you have no experience; this is part of the joy—and pain—of consulting. An answer like this signals to the interviewer that you are not comfortable working in this type of uncertain environment.

Good Answer

Candidate: So the question is how many pairs of jeans are purchased in the United States every year. There are a couple of ways of answering this question: one way would be to build from the ground up by estimating the jeans-wearing population and multiplying that number by the average number of new jeans each person buys each year. Another way would be to estimate the number of jeans that a single company makes each year and then multiply that by its market share. I'm going to try the first way because I think my estimates will be more accurate.

The candidate has given a preview of what she will be doing and also provided two ways of assessing the problem.

Candidate: Now, let's assume—for the sake of round numbers—that there are 250 million people in the United States. What percentage of the population buys jeans? Jeans seem to be a staple in most people's wardrobes, but for different reasons: for example, jeans are fashion statements for younger people, jeans are leisure and comfort wear for middle-aged people, and are functional for a large set of workers—mechanics, farmers, etc. I've even seen babies wearing jeans! They are also available in a range of prices, so no one is really priced out of the entire jeans market. I'd say, then, that about 80 percent of people wear jeans; this makes the total jeans market 200 million. The next step will be to determine how many pairs of jeans these 200 million people buy.

What the candidate has done well here is provide some insight into the jeans market and let that insight drive the assumptions. As a result, the candidate demonstrates some business savvy and intuition around customer behavior and price sensitivity. Also, note that the use of 80 percent results in a nice round number and that the candidate provides the interviewer with a roadmap of where she is going next.

Candidate: My guess would be that the average jeans-wearer has approximately three pairs of jeans. I recognize that there will be a large range: some people will only have one pair, others will have a quite a few, based on their needs and what they wear jeans for, but an average of three sounds about reasonable to me. Of course, if I was looking for exact market sizing, I would segment the market much more and see how many jeans each segment purchases.

Though the candidate is clearly guessing, this is okay as long as the interviewer is aware how you the candidate would get more detailed if she needed to.

Candidate: The next analysis involves estimating how often people buy jeans. Again, this is going to depend on what people are wearing jeans for: those who wear jeans for style and fashion are likely to replenish more quickly than someone who wears jeans around the house only. But again I'm going to take a guess and say that the average jeans last around three years. Therefore, people are buying new jeans every three years, and if they have three pairs of jeans each, it follows that on average they will be buying one new pair of jeans each year. So if the entire population of jeans wearers buys one pair of jeans each year, there are about 200 million new jeans bought each year.

The candidate has done a nice job of summarizing the logical steps and highlighting key assumptions.

Case 4

How many unique people attend events at the Rose Bowl every year?

This is an example of a question where you may have to ask the interviewer a couple of questions to develop a good response. Do not be afraid to ask questions, even when you are given a market-sizing analysis. Note also the simplifying assumptions that the candidate makes to avoid getting mired in a lot of messy numbers.

Bad Answers

- I don't know what the Rose Bowl is, so I'm uncomfortable answering the question.
  Don't show any trepidation about the question itself; you can figure it out!

- I don't like football.
  Where did this come from? All this shows is negativity; maybe the interviewer played in college.

Good Answer

Candidate: Well, I'm not really familiar with the Rose Bowl. I've heard of it, but I'm not sure exactly what it is and what it's used for. Can you give me a little more information?

Asking questions is perfectly fine, and the interviewer would rather have you ask a couple of questions than blindly start trying to figure out the question.

Interviewer: The Rose Bowl is a large outdoor stadium in Pasadena, California, that is used for sporting events (UCLA plays its home football games there, there are a few large soccer matches, and occasionally the Rose Bowl hosts the Super Bowl) and concerts. It holds about 100,000 people.

Candidate: Okay, well let's take the two types of events in turn. First, I'll analyze the sporting events. There is only one college football game per week, half of the games are away games, and the season is about 12 games. I'm going to assume that all the games are sold out. This means that there are six home games for a total of 600,000 people. Now, a lot of people will go to all the games—let's say 50 percent of the stadium is filled with repeat visitors. So this means that, for the first game, there are 100,000 different people, and that for each of the next five games there are 50,000 new people. Therefore there are 350,000 different people who go to college football games at the Rose Bowl.

The candidate has organized the analysis well, discussing the sporting events separately from the concerts. He has also highlighted the key to this case—that there are repeat visitors that must be factored out of the analysis to avoid double counting. Remember: don't worry if you don't know how many games are in a college football season; you will not get dinged for this!

Candidate: Now let's move to the soccer matches. I'm less comfortable with soccer, but let's give it a shot. I'm going to guess that over the course of the year there are ten soccer matches, and that each soccer match gets about 60,000 people, because the United States in general is less rabid about soccer than college football. However, soccer fans themselves are very loyal, so let's say that two-thirds of the people are the same for each game. This means that there are 60,000 for the first game, and 20,000 new people in each of the next nine games for a total of 240,000 people (60,000 + 180,000).

If the Rose Bowl holds the Super Bowl, it will definitely be packed. As a simplifying assumption, I'm going to assume that there is no overlap between the Super Bowl crowd and the college football or soccer crowd. There probably is overlap in reality, but it may be small because the Super Bowl attracts a national crowd. So this means another 100,000 people.

The candidate has made some logical assumptions, one of which may be a stretch but which simplifies the analysis. As long as the candidate acknowledges that the assumption is simplistic, the interviewer should have no problem with it.

Candidate: So now let's move on to the concerts. I'm going to assume that there are about 50 concerts in the Rose Bowl every year, roughly one a week. Some will sell out, others will not. Let's say that the average attendance at these concerts is 80,000. So this means that there are 4,000,000 people that go to concerts at the Rose Bowl. Unlike sporting events, you're probably not going to get a lot of repeat visitors, so let's say that there is no overlap with either college football, soccer, the Super Bowl, or other concerts.

Therefore, we have 4,000,000 from concerts, 350,000 for college football, 240,000 for soccer, and 100,000 when the Super Bowl is in town. So I'd guess that about 4,690,000 different people per year visit the Rose Bowl.

The candidate has successfully avoided getting too detailed, which would create headaches in tracking all the numbers.

Business Operations Questions

Case 5

A leading breakfast cereal manufacturer has hired you to determine why its profits have taken a dive in the last year. What should it do to improve its performance?

This is a typical case of declining profits. The interviewer is exploring the candidate's understanding of basic business concepts and the logical components of operating a manufacturing business.

Bad Answer

Candidate: Breakfast cereal is a bad market to be in. Customers who used to buy high volumes of cereal for their daily dose have changed their ritual to the Starbuck's model. Consumers now go to coffee shops and drink coffee with a muffin or bagel. Again, it is a bad market to be in. My hunch is that demand has taken a nosedive and our client is becoming very unprofitable as a result.

Slow down. This candidate is jumping in way too fast and drawing conclusions prematurely. The logic isn't terrible, aside from the fact that the interviewer specifically mentioned the problem being in the recent year and the coffee shop trend began many years ago. The candidate has missed a key piece of information, which will be costly.

Interviewer: Let's take this one step at a time. The problem our client is experiencing has surfaced within the past year. Demand for cereal hit a plateau a couple years ago. Given this information, how would you structure your diagnosis of the root cause or causes of this problem?

One more chance! The interviewer is nicely shooting down the candidate's hasty jump toward conclusion, and specifically asking for the candidate to show a structured diagnosis.

Candidate: Okay, so the issue isn't on the customer side. So if revenues are not at issue, then I would look at the manufacturer's costs. The commodity markets for cereal ingredients, such as corn and wheat, have gone up in the last year—I have a buddy who trades commodities for Goldman Sachs and makes a zillion dollars a year—and so I would imagine this client is taking a bath on raw materials.

Strikes two, three, and four. You're out! No one said the problem wasn't on the revenue side. What about competitors stealing market share? What about customer preferences changing? Additionally, the interviewer is assessing the candidate's knowledge of commodity markets and certainly doesn't much care about the friend's high-paying job at Goldman. Further, the candidate has quickly revealed his ignorance that complex manufacturing plants are more dependent on managing intense fixed costs than anything. Not to say variable costs aren't also critical. In any event . . . see ya!

Good Answer

Candidate: If profits have dropped, then either revenues have decreased recently, costs have increased, or both. Let's start with revenues. Has there been a drop in revenues recently? Specifically, have any changes in sales volumes or product pricing occurred, which would bring revenues down?

The candidate has shown that she understands the profit equation. She then proceeds by confidently diving into revenues. Also, she asks the question of revenue decline while at the same time demonstrating her understanding of its components, price, and volume. She may have scored additional points by mentioning potential reasons for price and volume changes, but she may be focusing on just gathering information up front, which is fine.

Interviewer: Yes, there have been changes to the client's revenue picture. Sales have dropped by 5 percent. Pricing has not changed.

Candidate: Okay, if pricing has not changed, then volume of cereal sales has declined. Let's explore this in greater detail. A decline in volume could be tied to a shrinking cereal market or to a reduction in market share. Perhaps the market for cereal is on the decline, say due to an increase in substitute products at coffee shops, for example.

She is staying true to her structuring by methodically investigating the problem. At this point, she begins to point out possible levers to shrinking volume. In doing this, she shows two high-level areas potentially responsible, namely market share or market size. Further, she presents a creative and logical rationale for why the market may be shrinking.

Interviewer: That's an interesting hypothesis. While the market for cereal has declined in the last 10 years, it leveled off last year and thus a shrinking market does not seem to be our problem here.

Candidate: So our client has been losing market share. Let's consider the reasons for this by looking at competitors and customers. Let's look at competitors first. Have competitors made any major strategic moves recently that may cause customers to buy their cereal over our client's? For example, they may have stepped up marketing efforts, improved existing products, introduced new products better aligned with customers, or lowered their pricing. Have any of these things occurred?

Good. She took the clue to skip market size and move to market share. In doing so, she presents logical reasons why share may be dropping. This is always smart because it serves a dual purpose of demonstrating creative hypotheses, while proactively getting the interviewer to steer you closer to the correct path. She also shows part of the three C's framework by looking at competitors.

Interviewer: Interestingly enough, no. Competitors have not done a thing, but have picked up market share as you mentioned. What about customers?

The interviewer has noted the candidate's consideration of competitors, and is now steering her toward customers to gauge her hypotheses.

Candidate: I would want to assess not only end consumers, but retail customers like supermarkets, mass merchants, and membership clubs. I would segment the end consumers first, to see if there has been a shift in preferences away from our client's cereal types toward those of its competitors, say from sugar to healthy cereals.

Excellent. The candidate highlights that there are two very different groups of customers, the stores that sell cereal and the end consumer of cereal. She also introduces a segmentation strategy, the cornerstone of many consulting problem-solving techniques. In doing this, again, she presents a potential rationale for a shift in consumer preferences.

Interviewer: The client has done extensive market research and found no changes in consumer preferences. In fact, our client's brand has been and remains on top in the minds of consumers. What would you look at regarding retail customers?

The interviewer continues to steer the candidate through the possibilities.

Candidate: Well, considering we have lost market share in a nonshrinking market in which consumers favor our product brand, pricing, and selection over competitors, we may have a supply problem. Have our retail customers had problems with the product supply coming from our client?

The candidate effectively summarizes what she knows so far, showing the interviewer that she is staying on track and is noting clues along the way.

Interviewer: Yes. Stock-outs have been increasing over the last year and retail customers have become agitated with orders frequently not being fulfilled by our client. Specifically, of the five cereal products produced by our client, it is only the "Amazing Flakes" line that is having problems. Unfortunately, this product is typically 60 percent of sales.

She is now on to something. But a bit of a curve ball has been thrown. The interviewer is now shifting away from the traditional drivers of revenue problems and toward the last of the three C's, the company and its operations. Further, the candidate is being asked to focus her analysis on one manufacturing line, most likely in the interest of time. This is undoubtedly meant to test the candidate's logic around manufacturing operations.

Candidate: Interesting. Okay, the revenue problem is neither customer nor competitor driven, but rather caused by our client's capacity to fulfill orders. Let's scrutinize our client's company to determine what the problem is. Not enough "Amazing Flakes" are being produced, so our client is capacity constrained. Either they have maxed out the production line's potential under efficient conditions and must expand, or something is going on with the line's efficiency. My hypothesis is that the line has stumbled in the last year, since we know that the size of the market has not grown and we assume that our client was able to supply enough "Amazing Flakes" in the past when the line was running well.

This is very good. The candidate shows an understanding of the two primary potential scenarios behind capacity problems. Better yet, she accesses earlier information about a flat market to hypothesize that the problem is one of efficiency and not plant size, since the client once could fulfill demand.

Interviewer: Good thinking. You are correct. Our client knows that expansion is not the answer, plus they are capital constrained as it is. They don't seem to be optimizing their plant's capacity on the Flakes line. Let's explore this. As you do, think about the capacity issue in terms of costs.

The interviewer is asking the candidate to directly talk about costs now. A very comprehensive case indeed!

Candidate: The cost structure of a manufacturing plant will be heavily weighted toward the fixed costs of plant and equipment, and therefore capacity utilization is key—especially if there is sufficient demand. We already know that there has been a drop in revenue, but given the link to our client's capacity problem, the cost per unit has undoubtedly risen because fewer units are being spread out across the fixed assets. Variable costs—raw materials, for example—should also be scrutinized. Has there been any change in variable cost per unit?

Good demonstration of her understanding of fixed and variable costs as they relate to a capital-intensive manufacturing plant.

Interviewer: You are correct about fixed costs. In fact, the "Amazing Flakes" line was running at 90 percent of its potential last year, but now is being utilized only 70 percent of the time. Variable costs have also gone up per outputted unit, while suppliers of rice, vitamins, and sweeteners have not raised the prices they charge to our client.

Careful here. Variable costs have gone up per box of cereal, but suppliers have not raised prices. The interviewer is seeing whether the candidate can speak immediately to this dynamic. Also, the utilization numbers clearly illustrate an efficiency problem, confirming that the candidate is on the right track.

Candidate: Hmm. The "Amazing Flakes" line is in serious trouble. I would want to conduct a full analysis of the three major aspects of a manufacturing line: Utilization, throughput, and quality. In other words, we want our client to be up and running as much as possible, we want as many boxes of cereal being produced per unit of operating time as possible, and of those units, we want as little waste as possible. With utilization first, we know that the machines are not running 30 percent of the time. This could be due to labor strikes or unscheduled downtime for maintenance. The rise in variable costs indicates that there is a lot of wasted raw materials. Perhaps the machines are not calibrated correctly. How is throughput?

The candidate has impressively showed her understanding of the three logical aspects of a manufacturing line. Again, she is taking clues given to her to present some hypotheses around utilization and quality. This will show the interviewer her creative thinking, while getting the interviewer to reveal which hypotheses are going in the right direction.

Interviewer: Throughput is normal. Talk to me more about utilization. You are right about the machines being down for maintenance more often. What could be happening?

Candidate: Well, the machines may have not been overhauled correctly, they may be just wearing down from age, or maybe the management of the line is less effective than it used to be.

Interviewer: Good point. There was, in fact, a management change last year on the "Amazing Flakes" line.

Candidate: That may be the driver. What changes in management approach occurred with the switch? How about maintenance? The new manager may be doing something different that is resulting in more downtime. Is all the maintenance reactive to a machine after it breaks or is any preventive maintenance down.

The candidate continues to aggressively investigate, while suggesting possibilities along the way. A good combination of techniques that will pay dividends in the mind of the interviewer.

Interviewer: Interesting question. The new manager ceased what he considered the excessive and costly preventive maintenance imposed by the previous manager. But this seems to be a problem since the line is broken 30 percent of the time now.

Candidate: Ah. Yes, it is a problem, but both managers could be correct to some extent. The new manager claims it is not economical to do "excessive" preventive maintenance. The previous manager imposed this kind of maintenance to avoid downtime. What I would do as their consultant is look at all machines on the line to determine failure history of each. I would also rank the level of impact each machine has on the line. I would institute regular and rigorous preventive maintenance on those machines with high-impact (i.e., those that single-handedly could result in line shutdown) and with high failure frequency. In that vein, I would avoid costly preventive maintenance on machines of lower criticality and less frequent mechanical problems. Ultimately, this will allow the client to maximize the value it draws from its fixed asset base in an environment of high demand.

The candidate respectfully hesitates to criticize the current or past decisions of client managers, and cleverly considers optimal and suboptimal aspects of both managers' maintenance strategies. The candidate displays a strong finish by taking the last clue and running with it toward a solid conclusion and recommendation. In doing so, she presents a logical framework of segmenting machines and ranking where each of them falls on scales of both impact and failure rate. She explains that it would be the results of this analysis that would guide the details of a final recommendation.

Case 6

A regional bank interested in expanding beyond commercial banking services has merged with a major asset management firm. They are struggling with post-merger integration and have hired you to help them. What issues would you address?

This question is less investigative in nature, but seeks to evaluate whether the candidate understands what challenges and critical areas a firm in a complex post-merger integration may face. The candidate is charged with structuring and displaying a comprehensive view of issues, as opposed to coming up with specific solutions.

Bad Answer

Candidate: I'll give it a shot, although I have absolutely no experience dealing with merger situations. Don't they usually bring in experts for something like this? I guess what I would do is make sure we get rid of excess people. Mergers are done for economies of scale and the only way to achieve that is to eliminate people. Certainly not a motivating thing for a consultant—I plan on focusing on growth strategy only. Anyway, I would also analyze competitors to make sure they are not trying to steal my customers during the transition period. I would also look at customers to ensure that they know what is going on and are not threatened by the merger in any way. So basically, my approach would use a three C's framework.

Not a strong beginning. No case is going to require that the candidate have situational expertise, but will be designed to see how the candidate thinks. This candidate wavers from the start and begins to make excuses right out of the gate. He also displays a limited view of what might motivate a merger other than to cut costs through economies of scale. A merger could be motivated by access to new customers, access to a specific expertise, geographical coverage, etc. Lastly, frameworks, when forced, will work against candidates. And never assume you know what kinds of cases you will be on. In a down economy, many of the cases done by operations and strategy consulting firms alike are cost-focused in nature.

Good Answer

Candidate: Interesting situation. Let me first give you a sense of how I would structure my approach, and then I will dive deeper into each issue. I would think about this challenge using both an external and internal perspective. Externally, I would consider the customer, first and foremost. I would also manage the impression by Wall Street regarding the merger. Internally, I would break my focus into five categories: organizational, cultural, technological, operational, and strategic.

The candidate lets the interviewer know how she plans on approaching the question. She lays out a simple, yet effective framework for considering the situation. She also lays out her planned areas of focus within both internal and external perspectives. This is valuable on two levels. First, it demonstrates thoughtful structure and gives the interviewer an opportunity to direct you down the most desirable path.

Interviewer: Sounds good. What would you think of first?

Candidate: I would think of the customer first. Depending on how communication has been handled to date, customers may not feel comfortable with the uncertainty that typically accompanies a merger. Risk of customer attrition must therefore be managed. Let's assume little has been done to date. I would first send announcements to my customers explaining the benefits of the merger and expressing our appreciation for their business. Some benefits may be bundled product offerings, access to a greater network of investment research, and better investment and banking rates. I would also have all relationship managers actively visiting and communicating with our most profitable customers. Finally, I may consider a brief survey to gauge customer concerns and preferences.

Smart to pick the customer first. All service businesses should start with the customer. She explains why there may be issues regarding customer satisfaction in the face of a merger, states an assumption, explains the business risk, and then proceeds to suggests several ideas to addressing the problem. Remember, this is not as much of an investigative case, such as a profitability case, and so this sequence of points is exactly what the interviewer is seeking.

Interviewer: That's great so far. Your earlier point about managing Wall Street is an important one, but let's move on to internal challenges. What issues would you address around culture?

The interviewer wishes to redirect the candidate toward an internal perspective and is satisfied with the candidate having mentioned, and briefly touched upon, the external issues. Points are scored and focus is achieved.

Candidate: With any luck, the architects of the merger carefully evaluated cultural mix before the merger was transacted. Unfortunately, this is often one of the least considered and analyzed factors in a pre-merger situation. I would take a similar path to that taken with my customers. Both formal and informal communication is critical, and expectations, hopes and concerns must be heard and addressed. Additionally, I would encourage all managers to informally meet with employees to gauge potential issues, as well as to communicate corporate strategy. This open communication will help to diagnose cultural issues as they surface. They can then be prioritized and addressed accordingly.

Without being overly presumptuous, the candidate demonstrates some knowledge of typical merger pitfalls and uses this knowledge to logically prioritize her discussion points. Further, as she introduces culture into the discussion, she begins by suggesting the gathering of information, both formally and informally. All effective consulting cases are predicated on gathering sufficient data first, even if the answer seems clear.

Interviewer: You mentioned technology. What would need to be done around technology?

The interviewer is not gauging technical expertise, but the logical connection between technology and a successful and profitable business, especially through a merger transition.

Candidate: I would imagine that there are complicated customer systems that help both companies manage their customers, track profitability, store transaction histories, execute transactions, and so on. Customers may even have access to proprietary account reporting software. Having some experience with financial services, I know that companies often have old legacy systems that are not easily integrated with other legacy systems. I would evaluate the strategic and operational significance of the systems that exist across the two firms and work with in-house technology experts to assess integration options. Technology is a critical part of a merger integration to get right, as any problems in transaction execution, balance reporting or customer information could damage the firm's credibility with clients, perhaps irreparably.

The candidate provides logical examples and draws from previous experience to assist in tackling the situation. As a result, she gains credibility in her views and demonstrates resourcefulness.

Interviewer: What about operational issues? Give me a couple examples of what you would address operationally.

The interviewer seems satisfied with her briefly addressing culture and technology, and now moves the candidate on to operational issues.

Candidate: The merged firm will have to meet the challenge of presenting a seamless, consolidated service for what previously were two customer groups, one commercial banking and one asset management. It will be critical that customers see the company as one and not as two separate companies sharing the same name. Relationship managers will need to be trained across products so they can look out for the best interest of their clients. Call centers will need to function cohesively and may have to be combined geographically. Call center reps will need to have efficient access to accurate customer information, as well as be trained on how to use that information. For example, it makes strategic sense to flag critical customers so call center reps can provide the appropriate level of service. To do this, it would be necessary to segment the new, combined customer group based on both current and future profitability.

The candidate continues to demonstrate the importance of looking through the customer's eyes. Good consultants must not be overly academic and inward-looking, but rather continuously take an "outside-in" perspective of the business. In doing this, she highlights a very important business point—and one that consultants frequently focus on—which is segmenting the "customer profitability gradient." Customers have varying levels of cost to support and subsequent levels of current and future profitability. These two sides of the customer equation must be used to prioritize a company's focus, as rarely are there enough resources to focus on all customers in the same way and with the same price points.

Interviewer: Yes, I agree. Good point. Since we are running short on time, briefly summarize remaining issues you would address.

The interviewer is satisfied and wants to wrap things up. The candidate has done well in moving through the question with structure and supporting detail. The interviewer wants her to broadly cover any remaining points—often an opportunity to obtain bonus points in the eyes of the interviewer.

Candidate: The organizational structure would need to be assessed. The merger is bound to result in overlap of functionality and a scenario of "too many cooks." Having complementary skill sets across the team would be a key objective. Also, it would be strategically important to analyze what products and services we want to emphasize most, so resources can be focused accordingly. And finally, if I was hired as a consultant to facilitate the integration, it would be absolutely critical to have a cross-functional merger task force made up of client employees dedicated to the effort. Our efforts would be governed by a strict project work plan, with clear timeframes and stated ownership.

Interviewer: Great job. That is a very comprehensive way to look at the problem.

Case 7

The owner of a hip college hangout called "Beer, Spaghetti and Exotic Desserts" recently hired a new manager and bartender to address a slump in customer volume. Customer volume quickly turned around, but the owner has noticed that profits have dropped. What is wrong?

This is an operations case dealing with declining profits. The interviewer has thrown in the additional twist of a business having strong customer volume at the same time as decreasing profits. The interviewer is assessing your ability to use a logical structure to methodically investigate the facts and uncover the solution.

Bad Answer

Candidate: Oh, that's very straightforward. The problem is linked to the beer. The owner relies on alcohol to make a profit, I'm sure, but most college kids are under age. So while the new manager and bartender have figured out a way to bring more butts to the stools, those butts are too young to buy beer. Also, why would anyone want to have exotic desserts with such options as beer and spaghetti? Exotic desserts are to be savored after elegant, exotic entrées. The strategy just doesn't make any sense to me.

Huh? The candidate entirely misses the point of demonstrating a structured thought process, by diving to an answer with careless assumptions and arrogant opinions. Remember, it's the journey and not the destination that the interviewer is most concerned about. In addition, this candidate does not logically address the question of why profits would go down despite the fact that, regardless of beer drinkers, more customers in the restaurant will undoubtedly result in a jump in revenues. So why are profits actually reversing? He misses this concept entirely.

Good Answer

Candidate: Sounds like an interesting hangout spot. Since profit equals revenue minus costs, I would approach the problem by scrutinizing the components of both. Let's tackle costs first, by considering both variable and fixed costs. Has there been a jump in rent, utilities, or employee compensation?

The candidate clearly lays out the profit equation—this should be automatic when receiving a profitability question. The candidate doesn't waver on where to start, but rather goes into costs, while at the same time demonstrating knowledge of cost components. Additionally, providing examples of specific cost items—as this candidate does—will win more points than simply asking if any costs went up, as it shows more comprehensive, proactive thinking.

Interviewer: Good thought, but no, rent and utilities are pretty much constant, and the owner is paying his new employees at the level of his previous ones.

Candidate: Let me assume that the costs of operating a restaurant are largely driven by the costs of ingredients. Has there been a change in unit costs for ingredients?

Consultants often have to make assumptions along the problem-solving path. You will win points as long as they are logical assumptions.

Interviewer: No.

Candidate: Okay. What about one-time, extraordinary expenses? For example, has there been any maintenance or construction done on the restaurant? Perhaps the owner purchased some new fixtures, tables, chairs, or cooking equipment.

Interviewer: There have been no one-time charges.

Candidate: Okay, let's talk about revenues. I would look at the two factors of revenue, namely volume and price. The new bartender and manager seem to have successfully brought in additional customers, so let's assume the volume of food and beer have gone up. What strategies have they implemented to do this? Perhaps they changed the product mix. Maybe the bartender has convinced the owner to carry more imported beers, for example, or the manager has added exciting new options to the food menu. Additionally, it is possible that prices have come down on certain food items to an extent that does not offset the volume jump.

The candidate is methodically moving through his framework, while expanding upon it as he digs deeper. Once a framework is presented, it is important to show the interviewer that you have discipline to stick with it. His thought process is very clear as he hypothesizes, demonstrates cause-and-effect logic, and probes for more information from an interviewer who has not revealed much.

Interviewer: No new drinks nor food items have been introduced. The owner believes that the bartender has partially driven new business due to his friendliness, drink-serving speed, and over-the-top enthusiasm. But the bulk of the new volume is being attributed to the manager having introduced an "all you can eat" strategy for its homemade spaghetti. Prices did change, but they went up for spaghetti to directly offset the additional cost of serving more spaghetti to each customer. Other than that, prices have remained the same.

Ah, a new menu strategy. A clue! Be looking for them and you will have better luck spotting them. They will always come and they will be deliberate. Careful of false clues, though. A lack of clues up to this point has been to test the candidate's patience and resolve in moving through the framework. A logical response to this clue would be that an "all you can eat" approach results in providing more food and thus raises costs. Note that the interviewer preempts this response by mentioning an offsetting price rise to the spaghetti special. This signals that he wants the candidate to dig deeper and think creatively.

Candidate: Okay. So we have determined no change in fixed or variable unit costs, no one-time charges, a jump in customer volume, and a raise in spaghetti prices to offset a the rise in cost for customers eating more spaghetti. Something definitely changed, as we still have a drop in profits. The additional volume is clearly driven by the perceived value of the "all you can eat" spaghetti offering. So we assume most customers were eating spaghetti and not other entrees offered. It is possible that the per-customer profit for other entrées is higher and therefore the owner is not enjoying the profits he may have seen before customers shifted to spaghetti?

The candidate efficiently scores on two levels here. First, he takes a step back to summarize what he has learned so far. This buys him time to think, while demonstrating that he is carefully and continuously considering all the evidence presented. He also shows logic in determining why volume has jumped, namely because of the menu change, while stating a further hypothesis around possible cannibalization of higher-margin entrées.

Interviewer: Good thought process. However, the margins on other entrées are the same or lower than that of the spaghetti. What else would you think about along those lines?

Again, the interviewer continues to present dead-ends in order to push the candidate's thinking. This is common among interviewers. Sometimes there may not even be an answer, but rather they just want to gauge your full capacity for coming up with additional hypotheses and ideas.

Candidate: You said they offered exotic desserts. How are the margins on the desserts?

Again, always be thinking about clues. The candidate has gone back to the very beginning of the case where the interviewer mentioned the name being "Beer, Spaghetti, and Exotic Desserts." Typically, a descriptive piece of information such as this is meant to help (and sometimes confuse) the candidate. Always be reflecting on and considering all pieces of information received along the way. If you are stumped, buy time by taking a timeout and summarizing what you know so far, as this candidate did earlier.

Interviewer: Good question. Dessert margins are extremely high. The dessert chef is highly skilled in exotic and artistically crafted desserts using inexpensive ingredients. Because of the uniqueness and quality of the desserts, the owner has found that customers are willing to pay high prices for them.

Candidate: Ah ha! There is your problem. An "all you can eat" offering of a food that is highly filling to begin with will result in nothing but extremely stuffed customers. When dessert rolls around—no pun intended—the customers will have no appetite to order high-margin desserts. As a result, I would advise the owner to remove the "all you can eat" strategy to bring customers back to eating high-margin deserts, even if it means a slight drop in volume.

Remember that the case should not end with the diagnosis of the problem, but with making a recommendation, even if obvious. You may also score bonus points by explaining what further analyses you would do if given more time. In this case however, little further analyses are needed.

Interviewer: Good job. That is exactly what the main problem was. Under further scrutiny, the owner found there to be one more problem with the business. Any thoughts on what else could be wrong?

Okay, the interviewer has noticed more time on the clock and has decided to push your thinking even further. Again, they tend to do this to measure your ability and appetite for pushing further, even when you feel you have arrived at a solution that seems good enough.

Candidate: How about beer? Alcohol is typically a high-margin item at any bar or restaurant. An increase in customers undoubtedly brought alcohol sales up. Was that the case?

Good. The candidate is not caught off guard, but rather jumps in with enthusiasm by making yet another logical point that extracts from clues in the initial case question.

Interviewer: Actually, no. Alcohol sales stayed the same, despite clearly more patrons sitting at the bar. Further, the owner's costs paid to alcohol suppliers went up, despite the distribution of customers across beer selections not changing.

Candidate: Well, it sounds like your bartender was very friendly indeed. He was likely giving away comp drinks as a courtesy to customers, without understanding the economic ramifications of his actions to the business.

Interviewer: Correct. Good job!

Case 8

The Director of Purchasing for the aircraft maintenance division of a major airline has asked for your help. His supplier base has grown to more than 500 vendors, who supply approximately 100,000 different aircraft parts to the airline. He has realized that his supplier strategy is suboptimal, both from a cost and efficiency standpoint. How would you help him devise a supplier strategy?

This is a supply chain case that digs deep into how a company should optimize its strategy around suppliers. It is meant to assess the candidate's business logic in a complex supplier environment with a large supplier base, providing parts which range from the very simple to the very complex.

Bad Answer

Candidate: Handling such tremendous volume of parts and suppliers can only be managed through technology. I don't mean this as a cop-out, but it's true. I am sure the client has some technology in place, but they likely need to bring in an IT consulting firm to analyze and install systems to create the best overall solution. Basically, the client should try to weed out a large portion of the suppliers. If the client gives more business to a smaller number of suppliers, they will charge the client less. So it's also about scale economies. Scale economies and technology. That really would help the client out significantly.

Careful of the technology trap. Technology is not a panacea. Aside from that, the candidate has missed the objectives behind case interviews. The interviewer wants to see a structured thought process. Sure, technology often plays a role in supply chain management, but this is not a technology question. The candidate needs to lay down a structure and then proceed with an analysis that illustrates strong business logic and demonstrates the way the candidate thinks. Scale economics is partly on the right track, but it would be more useful if the candidate elaborated with an example. Plus scale economics may not be relevant depending on types of parts and suppliers being considered.

Good Answer

Candidate: Wow, a lot of suppliers to handle, indeed! The first thing I would do is make sure I have all the necessary data consolidated in a database from which I can efficiently run spend analyses. From that I would segment the vast supplier base into manageable buckets from which to establish different purchasing strategies. An airplane is mixed with parts of different levels of criticality. The first bucket could consist of highly critical items linked to safety, such as navigation equipment, flight controls, and engine components. The second bucket could cover low-tech, commodity items such as basic nuts-and-bolts hardware, paint, wire, etc. The last bucket could contain items not critical to safety, but highly important to customer satisfaction, such as interior fabrics, seats, and in-flight entertainment systems.

Data management is critical given the scope of parts and the volume of suppliers who provide them. The candidate shows his understanding of this by suggesting the database. He then moves into his approach by discussing segmentation, both of parts and suppliers. This is a pervasive technique in consulting and critical to analyzing vast amounts of data. The candidate confidently settles on three "buckets" to work from and presents a logical rationale behind this segmentation. Overall, he is off to a good start by presenting a solid foundation from which to begin considering supplier strategies.

Interviewer: That seems like a good way to handle the mass of information. What would you do next?

Candidate: Once suppliers are segmented, I would establish decision criteria around what is important to the client in each of the three buckets. For highly critical items, logical criteria would be quality and reliability—cost would be secondary. Strong supplier support and priority service would also be important, so if an aircraft is grounded due to maintenance, they could be relied on to get it back flying as soon as possible. For commodity items, cost is a major concern. By definition, these items are straightforward to manufacture and can be bought from many different suppliers. The third bucket is trickier. The items are not safety critical, but will influence customers' desire to fly the airline over competitors, thus impacting revenue. Cost is a key criteria item, while ensuring innovative design that appeals to the customer.

Excellent. The candidate has gathered information, managed it through segmentation, and has now established decision criteria to guide strategy. He has thus presented a very structured approach that is logically sequenced. He has also linked supply-based decisions to the impact on revenues, namely grounded planes and customer choice.

Interviewer: That makes sense. Now what would you do?

Candidate: In each bucket I would next analyze the spend profile. Specifically, I would see how total costs are distributed across different parts and suppliers to understand what is driving the majority of my costs. This would allow me to focus my effort efficiently and not chase down cost reductions or quality enhancements for every part and every supplier, but rather just the primary ones.

These kinds of cases are very much about sifting through lots of data to pinpoint where the leverage is. His technique is correct. He is suggesting further segmentation within each parts category to identify the leverage. It is called the Pareto Principle—or more commonly, the 80/20 rule—and it refers to the common business fact that 80 percent of the value can be found in 20 percent of the factors, in this case it regards suppliers and parts.

Interviewer: That seems logical. Could you provide an example?

Candidate: Sure. Let's take the commodity bucket. Let's say that of 1,000 parts, I notice that 50 percent of total cost is spent on fuselage rivets, versus 1 percent on three-inch washers. I would thus scrutinize the suppliers of fuselage rivets and not washers. Then let's say that I see that 80 percent of the total spent on fuselage rivets goes to one supplier, whereas 20 percent goes to a remaining 24 suppliers of rivets. I may then focus any negotiating effort for a price reduction on the primary supplier and not all suppliers. An alternative strategy would be to tell all 25 suppliers that I am going to consolidate down to one primary and one secondary supplier of rivets. This would create a competitive bid situation, which will likely yield better pricing for our client. There would be great incentive for the suppliers to drop prices since they could win a large piece of our business, but also since picking up volume would lower their manufacturing costs by increasing capacity utilization and spreading out their fixed costs. I should note that the actual analysis would likely be more complex due to suppliers spanning across several different commodity types. Such a strategy may not work in other buckets if suppliers are differentiated, there are few suppliers, or switching costs are high for our client.

Always be prepared to elaborate with an example and to illustrate with numbers. Interviewers love it. It demonstrates further analytical horsepower. The candidate clearly illustrates the concept of the 80/20 rule here. He also shows an understanding of potential negotiating tactics available, given the example. In doing this he demonstrates a win-win approach by suggesting a supplier would have the incentive to lower prices, win more volume, and therefore benefit by covering more of its fixed costs. Additionally, being unsure of whether time is running out in the interview, he scores extra points by suggesting added complexity requiring consideration in a real life situation. If the interviewer wants more on that added complexity, he will ask for it and it won't be a strike against the candidate. Finally, he clearly points to drivers of the buyer-supplier balance of power, recognizing that strategies will differ depending on that balance.

Interviewer: You seem to have a good grasp of controlling supplier costs. You have laid out a good "buy for less" strategy for commodity suppliers. What other strategies might you consider to improve efficiency and cost across all buckets?

The interviewer seems content with the one strategy example for a specific bucket, and now wants to push your thinking further on general supplier optimization strategies that span all buckets.

Candidate: Inventory management is a critical factor across all buckets. If our client is out of stock of parts when they need them, it could result in costly grounded planes. Additionally, having too much inventory on hand results in high carrying costs. I would work closely with primary suppliers to ensure that the latest inventory management techniques, such as just-in-time and vendor-managed inventory, are in place. Technological tools can also be leveraged to improve coordination with suppliers, demand forecasting accuracy, logistical flows, and transactional efficiency. Also, if our client is part of an airline consortium, it would be valuable to leverage their overall buyer power and share best practices regarding supplier management. Lastly, I would involve suppliers in future solution design decisions to drive toward more standardization, simplified specifications, and rationalized requirements.

A discussion around supply chain is not complete without some mention of controlling the flow and timing of goods to the buyer. This candidate seems to have an additional grasp of some of the techniques out there, such as JIT and VMI (this terminology would not really be expected). Such complex supply chains will undoubtedly rely on effective use of technology to manage them. The candidate sees this, which will score him points, as well. Finally, the candidate goes above and beyond by speaking to the potential advantages of leveraging airline consortiums and involving suppliers as partners in design decisions—again a win-win perspective.

Interviewer: Good job.

Nailing the Case

Business Strategy Questions

Case 9

A small manufacturer and distributor of women's surf clothes is considering selling to high-end boutiques and has hired you to help out. What kinds of issues would you think about to help it make the decision?

This is a case about entry into new channels; the issues are similar to market entry cases.

Bad Answer

Candidate: Selling surf clothes in high-end boutiques seems like an absurd idea. I've never seen them in any boutiques I've been in. I'd tell the client not to do it.

What is the analysis based on?

Interviewer: Well, the client is fairly serious about it. The average selling price is much higher in boutiques than it is in surf shops, so it may represent an interesting opportunity.

The interviewer is giving the candidate a very clear hint, and is also providing her with some data that she will want to factor into your analysis. In these cases, take the hint and reconsider.

Candidate: Yeah, but I still don't think that it's a good idea. I just don't think that surf clothes and boutiques match. I bet if I talked with a bunch of my friends, they'd all say the same things.

The candidate has not taken the hint, and the interview is essentially over. It's important to avoid starting with a strong bias as you go into a case.

Interviewer: Oops! I forgot that I scheduled a conference call during this time. Maybe we could reschedule.

Or maybe not.

Good Answer

Candidate: I hate to sound overly structured, but I think the 3C framework will work nicely here, and help me to organize my thoughts and analysis. So I'll discuss the customer, the competition, and the company in that order. First, let's talk about some information that I would need about customers. Do people who shop at surf shops also visit boutiques? Or is the client trying to attract a new base of customers by selling through boutiques? In essence, what is the target market for both the surf shops and the boutiques and how do they overlap or differ? This would answer questions about cannibalization of the existing customer base.

This is a good use of a framework to set up the answer. When you so apply an off-the-shelf framework like the 3Cs, be sure that it is appropriate. Interviewers tell us that they really dislike it when candidates struggle to bend a problem to an ill-fitting framework.

Interviewer: Okay, so you would want to know about who is buying the clothes. In the apparel industry, there are really two sets of customers: the retailers and the consumers. What type of information would you want to know about the retailers?

The interviewer is leading the candidate down a specific path, so by all means she should follow it!

Candidate: Ah, good question, I need to consider the channel. First off, I'd want to know something about the size of the boutique market: is it big enough to sustain a new product introduction? Also, what are the economics of serving the boutique market? And, perhaps most importantly, would they be interested in buying our product? Is surf wear "in"?

Interviewer: All good questions. It turns out that the average selling price of clothing at boutiques is significantly higher than at surf shops—this shouldn't surprise anyone. Also, beach wear in general is "in" right now, and the client has a fresh, youthful brand. What concerns the boutiques, though, is price competition from other retailers: they do not want to see a piece of clothing that they sell at their store for sale at a surf shop for two-thirds the price. How does this impact the decision?

The interviewer is taking an active role in leading the discussion, even though he is starting to take the candidate away from his framework. Remember: being too rigid in your frameworks is almost as bad as using the wrong framework. It's doubtful that you will ever be able to march all the way through an interview by sticking to the same framework. Use it as a crutch when you get into trouble, but rely primarily on the interviewer—not the framework—to guide you.

Candidate: Well, the margins seem to be pretty good at the boutiques, assuming that costs to serve are relatively similar for surf shops and boutiques. And our brand and type of clothing seem to fit with their needs. The question will be avoiding channel conflict. There are a couple of ways to get around this. One is to simply avoid geographical overlap by selling to boutiques in one geography and surf shops in another. Another is to create a new line of clothing that is branded separately from the clothing the client sells to surf shops.

Interviewer: Good. What else would you want to know?

Now is the time when the candidate can get back to her framework. The interviewer is clearly satisfied with this line of analysis and is ready to move on.

Candidate: I would want to know about the competition. What types of surf clothing exist in boutiques now? This would help the client assess share of wallet at the boutiques and assist in profitability analysis. Also, what type of competition exists in surf shops? And what is the nature of that competition: is it based on price, fashion, fit, quality, or other factors? If the client is successful in moving into boutiques, who is going to follow? Can the client establish any barriers to entry?

Interviewer: What type of barriers to entry are you thinking about?

Be careful which buzz words you use when using frameworks because interviewers will pounce on them and see if you know what you're talking about or if you're blindly trying to impress him.

Candidate: I was thinking about things such as a strong sales force, exclusive agreements, production scale.

Hopefully the candidate was actually thinking about these things. . . .

Interviewer: You mentioned the nature of the competition. How would you test whether or not the competitive environment within this new channel would be the same as the traditional surf shop channel?

Candidate: There may be examples of other channel expansions within the apparel industry that I could take a look at, but my operating assumption would be that because the same set of competitors would be involved, the nature of the competition would be the same.

Interviewer: Good. I want to touch upon how the company's operations would change to serve this new channel. What type of new capabilities do you think they would need to add?

The interviewer, again, is taking an active role in structuring the interview, and it's the candidate's role to take the lead.

Candidate: Well, I mentioned the sales force earlier. Because the buyers are likely different, the client would probably have to develop a new sales force targeted at this new channel. These sales representatives would need to have a broader understanding of fashion trends and not just specialize on surf apparel trends. In addition, design and manufacturing processes may need to change—perhaps the boutiques require a different type of merchandise with more emphasis on fashion than on function. And, the client would need to assess capacity requirements: can existing capacity be used? Or do new plants need to be built?

Interviewer: Good analysis. Now let's talk a bit about your resume.

Case 10

Your client is a large owner and operator of hotels and vacation properties. It also runs a highly successful rewards program that gives guests the opportunity to earn points for each stay. The company is considering partnering with small bed-and-breakfasts and offering guests the opportunity to earn points for stays at participating B&Bs as well. Should it go ahead with this partnership? What should it think about in order to make its decision?

This is a classic strategy question: how to grow and how to grow profitably? There's clearly a lot of information missing, so half of the problem will involve getting the right information out of the interviewer.

Bad Answer

Candidate: Chances are that a lot of hotel chains have looked at this as an opportunity, and because they haven't done it, my inclination would be to say that it's probably not a good idea.

Don't lead off with a conclusion, because what the interviewer is looking for foremost is the thought process and logic for dissecting the question.

Interviewer: I don't know if that's true, but even if it is, the client believes that it has some strong competitive advantages that might make it successful.

The interviewer is leading the candidate to the trough, hoping he will drink!

Candidate: But there are thousands of B&Bs out there—there's no way that the client could sign up all of them, and only signing up a few would not be worth the time. The execution of the strategy would be very difficult.

The candidate has skipped to talking about the implementation and, while important, it is not the focus of the question. He also has not taken the clue and is going to have a very difficult time recovering to save himself.

Good Answer

Candidate: Well, we're going to want to weigh the advantages of such a program against its costs and risks. First, I'd like to ask a couple of questions. First, what types of customers does the client target? Second, what types of hotels does the client operate? And third, I want to get a sense of how the proposed partnership might operate; I need to address what the revenue and cost structure would look like.

This is a much better and safer approach. The candidate has set up a loose framework (cost-benefit analysis) and has probed for more information. It's a good rule of thumb to force yourself to ask a question of your interviewer after hearing a case. It will almost never hurt you to do so, and will allow you a little more time to prepare your own thoughts.

Interviewer: Let me answer the third question first. The way the program would work—and it's your job to determine if there are any other ways to structure the flow of funds—is that each B&B would pay the client an annual membership fee to be part of the network. Customers would then be able to earn reward points each time they stayed at the B&Bs, and also redeem their points at these participating B&Bs. In return, the client would provide them with access to the centralized reservation service and allow them to advertise the fact that they are part of our network.

Candidate: And would members of the reward program be able to stay for free at the participating B&Bs?

This question demonstrates understanding of the program and shows that the candidate has been listening attentively.

Interviewer: Good question. That's up for discussion. Now you also asked some questions about the customer base. What specific information are you looking for and why do you want to know about it?

Beware of asking questions only to fill time. Interviewers want to know that you're thinking before you're talking.

Candidate: What I'm looking for there is a sense of overlap between the customers in the reward program and those who visit B&Bs. We need this to get a rough estimate of demand.

Interviewer: I see. The client owns and operates higher end hotels that are primarily used for business purposes. The average customer is wealthy, lives in the suburbs, and travels significantly. The customer base is highly loyal and redeems points on vacations. Moreover, the customer plans vacations around his or her ability to redeem points for free stays; as an example, a customer will go to Park City instead of Vail for a ski vacation if he or she is able to stay for free.

The interviewer has revealed a lot of information about customers and customer preferences. It's important to note that some of the data that the interviewer gives you will be more relevant than others; it's your responsibility to sift through it.

Candidate: Interesting. Because the customers are redeeming their points on vacation, I'm going to assume that they're not currently staying at B&Bs, because they can't redeem their points there. But would they stay at B&Bs if they could, or are they so used to large hotels and all of the modern amenities that are associated with them that these customers would not stay at B&Bs?

This is the appropriate time to start making assumptions; the candidate has demonstrated an understanding of the situation and has asked a lot of questions. Something to think about: If you're halfway through your allotted time and you're still only asking questions, you may want to think about initial conclusions to focus your analysis and line of questioning. The interviewer will challenge your assumptions if she disagrees with them.

Interviewer: Another good question. The client recently conducted a survey that said that customers are seeking less adventurous vacations and are staying closer to home. They prefer a quieter, more removed setting.

Candidate: Which is what a B&B offers, I imagine. So there is demand for the program, at least from the existing base of reward program members.

The candidate has established a lot of credibility with the interviewer by immediately incorporating the information given and linking it to her line of logic.

Interviewer: It appears so.

This is a critical time in the interview. The candidate has made some initial conclusions, but the interviewer is not going to provide guidance on where to go next.

Candidate: But what we must also consider is whether or not there would be demand for the B&Bs for this program. Reward program members, it seems, would only be staying at B&Bs if they could stay for free by using points, so the B&B owners would be providing a room for free. If all they get from the client is access to a reservation system, which we've already established wouldn't be that useful if the B&B is only being used for free stays, it doesn't sound like a very compelling value proposition.

This is a nice summary of how a B&B owner might react to the proposed partnership arrangement and also shows that the candidate remembers the structure of the program that the interviewer gave at the outset.

Interviewer: I agree. But from our client's perspective, I hear you saying that it may be an attractive program because it responds well to customer priorities. What could our client do with the structure of the program to make it more attractive to the B&Bs?

The interviewer is clearly impressed with the candidate's analysis thus far and has asked her to consider restructuring the initial proposal. If you get into these types of details during a case interview, it's a signal that you've done very well.

Candidate: Well, the client is going to have to make the financials much more attractive to the B&B owners. The client could reimburse the B&B owners for the cost of the room or pay the B&Bs an annual fee instead of vice versa. Of course, these costs would need to be weighed against the revenue the client would receive for offering the program, which is the estimated increase in number of paid stays at the client's hotel network.

There are a lot of other potential adjustments to the program: for example, midweek stays only when the B&Bs are likely not at capacity (and therefore not losing marginal revenue), requiring a three-night minimum where the customer pays for two nights, and so on. Don't make a laundry list; the interviewer would rather hear how you would analyze whether or not your idea will work.

Interviewer: Great. Let's move on to another case.

Case 11

A camera company has stumbled on a compound that helps extend the life of cut roses. It wants to know if it should introduce the product and how to price it. The firm has collected the following data and wants your assistance in analyzing the data and making a recommendation:

- One billion roses are purchased each year in the United States.
- The average rose costs $2.
- There are 50 million unique buyers of roses.
- The chemical extends the life of cut roses by one week.
- There are five other products on the market that extend the life of cut roses from two to five days.
- Five grams per rose of the new chemical must be present in order to be effective.
- It costs $0.02 per gram to manufacture the new chemical, including fixed and variable costs.

Pricing cases are very common. It is also common that the interviewer will give you a lot of information upfront. If the interviewer doesn't give you a sheet of paper with the data, make sure you write it down. Also, understand that there is likely going to be more data that you're going to need to gather as you go along. Because the interviewer is specifically asking for the price of the product, you're going to need to perform a pricing analysis, based on the benefit created by the product and an estimate of how much of the benefit the company can capture.

Bad Answer

Candidate: The market is $2 billion, which seems pretty big to me. However, it's a camera company we're talking about, and they probably don't have a lot of experience in this area, so maybe they should consider selling the product to someone with more experience.

It's always dangerous to jump to conclusions so quickly. The interviewer has given the candidate a lot of information, and obviously expects him to do more with it than multiply the number of roses by the average cost of the rose. And though it might be a good idea to talk about execution, leave this to the end of the discussion.

Interviewer: Interesting thoughts, but I'd like to focus on the viability of the product and its price. Does the data shed any insight into whether the client should commercialize it?

The candidate is getting one more chance.

Candidate: Okay. There are five competitors out there, which is a lot, and our product is only marginally better than theirs, so it's going to be pretty tough to get share without really lowering the price, so I don't think that it's going to be profitable.

Snap judgments are never a good idea. Real clients pay consultants a lot of money to be thoughtful. This interview is over.

Good Answer

Candidate: Before we get to pricing, I want to talk about market sizing: is the market big enough to be attractive? If the market is attractive, then I'll talk about pricing and, since you gave me cost information, we can talk about profitability. If the product is viable, then we'll investigate what the competition looks like and whether or not the company has the capabilities to execute.

A nicely structured overview. Note that there is a decision tree here: if the market is big enough and the product is profitable, then the candidate will discuss the competitive environment and implementation.

Interviewer: Sounds good to me.

Candidate: First, the market size. The annual market size is $2 billion, which is certainly not small. Do we have any idea about growth rates?

Interviewer: The cut roses market has been growing at about 5 percent per year and is expected to continue to do so.

Candidate: Okay, so we have a pretty large market with solid—if not spectacular—growth. Seems too big to ignore. So I'll move onto the profitability of the product.

As a rule of thumb, market sizes in strategy questions will always be big enough. Otherwise, the case ends here and the interviewer will not get any real insight into the candidate's analytical skills.

Candidate: The way I'm going to approach the pricing of the product is to assess how much value our product creates for customers, and then use the data you gave me about value capture to determine the price. The benefit that the product creates for customers is that it extends the life of cut roses by a week. To quantify the benefit, though, I need to know the percentage increase in life: what is the average life of cut roses without any chemical supplement?

The candidate is thinking out loud and explaining exactly where he's going. This gives the interviewer a chance to see the candidate's logic and redirect if necessary.

Interviewer: About a week.

Candidate: Okay, so we're essentially doubling the life of the roses. I'm going to assume, therefore, that we're doubling the "value" of the roses to the customer, though this may be overstating things because the perceived value to the customer may decrease over time. Now I need to get a sense of the current "value" of the roses to the customer to quantify the delta. From the data you gave me, there are 50 million buyers of roses buying one billion roses, or 20 roses per buyer. Each buyer is spending $40 on roses per year, which I can equate to be the perceived value. If the chemical is doubling their value, then the new perceived value of roses per buyer per year will be $80. The value the product is creating is $2 per rose. These numbers seem a little strange—how am I doing?

A little advice: It's okay if the analysis that you're doing seems a little awkward to you and the numbers a little out of whack. The interviewer is testing your ability to manipulate a data set. But if you feel uncomfortable, check in with the interviewer, like the candidate has done here.

Interviewer: I think your assumption that we're going to double the value of the roses is a little off. The client has done a little research and found out that by doubling the life of the rose it only creates about $0.50 of value per rose. Most of the perceived value to the customer is wrapped up in buying the roses and enjoying them for the first couple of days.

Remember, this is a two-way street. The interviewer is there to help you and will appreciate your sanity checking your own analysis.

Candidate: That feels a little better to me. So the product could theoretically be priced at $0.50, assuming that the client is able to capture all of the value created by the product. But this is probably unlikely. Are there other examples of recently introduced products that could be used as benchmarks?

The candidate is suggesting a means to gauge price range for the product by conducting a specific analysis. This will resonate strongly with the interviewer.

Interviewer: Products that have been priced in the manner you are suggesting— "value pricing"—have captured anywhere from 25 percent to 75 percent of the value they create.

Candidate: Okay, let's take the average and assume that our product will capture 50 percent of the value. So we price it at $0.25 per rose.

Interviewer: And what does this imply about the profitability of the product?

Candidate: Well, it costs $0.02 per gram to make the chemical, or $0.10 to create enough chemical to sustain one rose. This means that our margin would be about $0.15 per rose.

Interviewer: Are there other costs that we need to consider?

This is certainly a leading question—the answer is going to be a categorical "yes."

Candidate: Ah, you gave me manufacturing costs. There are probably distribution costs, packaging, sales, and indirect costs that are going to be associated with the product. Do we have an estimate on what those might be?

Interviewer: All other costs are another $0.02 per gram.

Candidate: So now we're up to costs of $0.20 per five grams. This makes our margin $0.05 per 5 grams, or 20 percent. The profitability seems viable, so now we need to consider the competitive environment. You mentioned five other competitors. Can you tell me anything more about the individual competitors or the nature of the competition?

The candidate has wrapped up the profitability analysis and made the logical jump to talking about the competitive environment, consistent with your initial framework. At this point, he is probably a little tired from the profitability analysis, so it's a good time to ask an open-ended question.

Interviewer: Competition is fierce. The largest competitor has well-established distribution agreements and a strong brand. It has a history of engaging in price wars. In fact, prices of similar products have fallen 30 percent over the last year and several other companies have exited the market.

Candidate: Well, this doesn't sound too promising. And, given that the client is a camera company and may not have any experience with this type of product or the market, maybe it's not such a good idea to enter the market. Plus, it may distract management attention from other, more core products.

The new information about the competitive environment does indeed change the analysis. The candidate has done a good job of incorporating it quickly into his own thinking; it's also always a good idea to discuss the opportunity cost of a new product or service, as he's done here by mentioning management focus.

Interviewer: I agree. But at the same time you've concluded that it's a potentially profitable product. Can you think of ways the client could capture any of the value or is it a lost cause?

Again, a leading question. The interviewer is testing the candidate's creativity.

Candidate: Well, one idea might be to sell the product to an existing player. Another might be to go after different customers—for example, sell it to flower store owners. And a third idea might be to invest in research to see if the product has any other uses.

The candidate has passed the creativity test nicely.

Interviewer: Good thinking. I think you did a fine job on the case.

Case 12

Your client is a large private equity firm. It is looking into "rolling up" the tow-truck industry; that is, buying many small- and medium-sized firms and combining them to create one, larger firm. It wants your help in assessing industry attractiveness.

Don't be intimidated by the jargon. This is a classic industry attractiveness question and should be treated as such.

Bad Answer

Candidate: I'm going to use the 3C framework for this case: company, competition, and cost. First, I'm going to talk about the existing tow truck companies, then the competition between them, and finally the cost of purchasing the individual firms.

The candidate has awkwardly tried to apply a framework that doesn't work in this case. The 3C framework should be used for new market opportunity questions, which is not the case in this example. The interviewer is going to be wary.

Interviewer: What the client really wants to know about is the attractiveness of the industry; you've mentioned a couple of the aspects, but I didn't hear anything about customers or barriers to entry. Should we be considering those things as well?

This is one nice interviewer. She is almost spoon-feeding the candidate a framework, which the candidate should easily recognize.

Candidate: I'll get to that at the end; I've never been a consultant before, so I'm not too familiar with the frameworks. The 3C framework is one that works for me, so if you don't mind I'm going to stick with it, even though it might be a little messy.

Hopefully the candidate didn't make quotation marks with her fingers when she said "framework." Interviewers are looking for your ability to be flexible and comfortable with new problems. Don't force-fit a framework.

Good Answer

Candidate: The client has asked me to assess industry attractiveness. This seems like a pretty good opportunity to use Porter's Five Forces. So I'm going to follow that framework. First, the buyers: what is the relative power of customers? Well, when you get your car towed, you certainly feel powerless!

Humor is a little risky, but may break the ice a bit if you think the interviewer will enjoy the levity.

Candidate: I do think, though, that this is important. Customers need to get their car back, and must pay the exorbitant fees that are required to get their car out of the lot. In addition, they are somewhat price insensitive and willing to pay whatever it takes to retrieve their car. So, from a bargaining power of suppliers' perspective, the industry is fairly attractive.

The candidate has given a brief—but effective—overview of one of the Five Forces and come to a logical conclusion. Analysis of all of the categories can take a while, so it's to your benefit to move quickly and let the interviewer stop you in areas where she wants more analysis.

Interviewer: Sounds good to me. What's next?

Candidate: Let's talk about the bargaining power of suppliers. Again, I don't see suppliers having a lot of bargaining power over the tow truck firms. I'm defining the suppliers as the companies that make the tow trucks. I'm also assuming that there are several manufacturers of those trucks. Is this correct?

Interviewer: That's a good assumption. There are quite a few firms that manufacture tow trucks.

Candidate: What about labor? Are there unions that I need to be concerned about?

Interviewer: How does this relate to suppliers?

Candidate: Well, if one union supplies all of the labor, for example, it will be able to exercise a significant amount of control over the labor force, which is one of the key "supplies" that a tow truck firm needs to operate.

The candidate has demonstrated a broad understanding of supplier power.

Interviewer: In the geography where the client is looking to roll up the industry, there are no unions.

Candidate: Okay. So, similar to buyer power, there doesn't seem to be a lot of supplier power in this industry.

It's a good idea to summarize whenever you come to the end of a line of logic and, when relevant, relate it to other conclusions that you've drawn during your analysis. This gives you a chance to take a breath, and also gives the interviewer a window to ask follow up questions. If the interviewer does not ask any questions, you can feel confident that you are doing a good job thus far.

Interviewer: I agree.

In this case, silence is golden.

Candidate: Next, I'm going to tackle barriers to entry. High barriers to entry may mean large initial capital investments, complicated technology, complex manufacturing processes, or regulatory barriers. Now let's see if any of these apply to the tow truck industry. In terms of capital requirements, new entrants certainly need a couple of trucks. In addition, the new firm would need access to real estate to store the vehicles once they are towed. Can you tell me how this works? Do firms own their own storage lots? Lease them? Are there central lots?

The candidate has given a nice definition of barriers to entry and is now addressing them in turn. This demonstrates an understanding of the concept and the ability to take a piece of the framework and apply it. It also helps the candidate organize her thoughts. And remember: ask questions!

Interviewer: The answer is yes. Some own their own lots, others lease. But the majority of vehicles are taken to central lots owned by the municipality. All vehicles that are towed from city streets are taken to these central lots, and you have to have a contract with the municipality in order to bring vehicles there.

Notice how a simple question has revealed some significant insights into how the industry operates. The interviewer is rewarding the candidate for asking the right questions.

Candidate: So the vehicles that are brought to other locations have been towed off privately held property?

Interviewer: Correct. As an example, if you get your car towed from a mall parking lot, it will be brought directly to the towing company's lot.

Candidate: Okay, so we've just identified another barrier to entry—having a contract with the city. How hard is it to get these?

Interviewer: They're not easy to come by, and you have to pay the municipality an arm and a leg to have access to these central lots.

Candidate: Interesting. So this is a pretty significant barrier to entry, which, from our client's point of view, makes the industry fairly attractive.

The candidate is thinking about what the analysis means for the client. Whenever possible, think about client implications and state them clearly and explicitly.

Interviewer: Good. I think we've done a good job of thinking about barriers to entry.

A sign to move on.

Candidate: We still have to talk about substitutes and competition. Let me address substitutes first. Here, I think the industry is going to be less attractive to the client because towing is really a commodity business. There is certainly no brand loyalty, and little differentiation between the services provided: in the mind of the customer, one tow truck company is the same as another.

This analysis is fairly straightforward, and the candidate has done a good job of hitting the high points without going into too much detail.

Interviewer: Makes sense to me; I've never heard of someone talk about brand loyalty and tow truck companies in the same breath.

A consultant's feeble attempt at humor.

Candidate: Finally, we get to competition, or rivalry among firms. Based on the analysis of substitutes that I just did, I imagine that there is a lot of competition because the product is not unique.

Interviewer: What type of competition, specifically?

Candidate: For commodity products, competition typically revolves around price.

Interviewer: But you mentioned at the beginning of the case that buyers are fairly cost insensitive.

The interviewer has moved into a different mode and is now challenging the candidate. If you get into one of these situations, do not take this as a sign that you are doing poorly. The interviewer is trying to see how you react to a more direct line of questioning. Just keep your cool.

Candidate: I think in this case the price competition would mostly be around how much the tow truck companies would pay for the right to tow. We mentioned the contracts with the city earlier, but I imagine that tow truck companies must pay for access to vehicles that are towed from malls, accident scenes, etc.

The candidate has kept his cool and explained exactly what he means about price competition. The candidate has also made some reasonable assumptions about how the industry might work——even if it is completely off, the logic is rational, and this is all the interviewer cares about.

Interviewer: I see what you mean, though isn't this at some level a discussion of supplier power since these industry participants are supplying the tow truck companies with the right to tow?

The interviewer is now playing "bad cop" and trying to fluster the candidate by telling him that he forgot about a key supplier. This will happen: don't worry about it.

Candidate: Yeah, I guess you're right. I'm glad we at least got to it, though.

Interviewer: So what does this mean for our client?

Candidate: It means that the industry—at least from a competitive point of view—is unattractive. So if I can summarize, the industry is attractive from a buyer power and barrier to entry perspective. It is less attractive in terms of substitutes, competition and, in light of the analysis we just did, supplier power.

Interviewer: So, what would you tell the client?

Candidate: Overall, the industry is unattractive and the client should not seek to roll up the industry.

To the interviewer, the final conclusion is much less important than the subsequent analysis.

Resume Questions

Case 13

After one year with our firm, what would our formal evaluation of your performance look like?

This is merely a creative way of asking the very typical interview question regarding your strengths and areas of improvement. The twist is responding creatively, while having some perspective of a timeframe that is a year away. Resume questions primarily aim to gauge your fit within the culture of the organization. Assessing the poise and maturity with which you answer this question is a classic way to measure fit. Additionally, make sure to know the "between the lines" messages of your resume in anticipation of what they may already suspect as a gap with the requirements of an effective consultant in their particular firm.

Bad Answer

Candidate: Comprehensive strengths, no weaknesses! Just kidding. Seriously though, my evaluation would be focused around strengths. It would highlight my superiority in structuring financial analyses, my position at the top of my consulting class, and my ability to tee-up future business opportunities with senior clients. It would also express my strong ability to solve complex quantitative and qualitative problems. As for weaknesses, they wouldn't be around skills so much. I guess I am a perfectionist. I also find it frustrating to problem solve with a group of people. Too many cooks and too inefficient! I am at my best blazing ahead on my own.

Yikes! Cocky humor is risky and will turn people off. Arrogance is unimpressive, even if you perceive your interviewer to be a tad arrogant. Confidence and a positive tone are most effective. With his attitude of superiority, this candidate would quickly alienate his colleagues anyway, which deteriorates firm culture. He has also expressed ignorance toward the job description. No fresh MBA or undergrad is going to directly sell future business opportunities with senior clients. Their role is to provide good consulting results in order to open the door for partners to discuss future opportunities. Oh, and please, please either don't use the "perfection-ist" line or find a better way of saying it. Finally, when discussing areas of development (don't call them weaknesses), talk to addressable items and not deeper personality issues that directly conflict with the nature of consulting.

Good Answer

Candidate: That's a very interesting question. For sake of argument, let me start by briefly laying a foundation of consulting activities I may be evaluated on during that first year. Given my four years' experience at Merrill Lynch, my desire to stay involved in financial services as a consultant, and the increasing operations and strategy work your firm is doing in this space, let's assume this area of activity for my case work.

The candidate does a good job at laying some context with logical assumptions that have the additional benefit of illustrating his knowledge in the kind of work the firm does. He immediately displays a structured approach, even with a somewhat conversational resume question.

Candidate: Let me cover strengths first. First, I am confident that my evaluation would highlight creative thought leadership. Given my experience in financial services and the nature of the project-oriented work I did at Merrill, both in operations and strategy, I will be proficient in finding leverage points and framing the resulting implications in a language the client understands. Also, it will highlight my strong ability for identifying actionable solutions. I spent a year leading a special-project team in Merrill's fixed income operations group, which was very successful due to laying out actionable steps, while effectively managing the 80/20 rule. Finally, my evaluation would highlight my strength in client relations. I enjoy working with people and have effectively interacted with people across many functions and levels in my past experiences.

This is something I will thrive at in serving consulting clients. I believe these strengths will make me a strong contributor to your firm, as consultants need to think creatively, recommend actionable solutions, and have strong rapport and credibility with clients.

The candidate does a great job on many levels. He starts with the strengths first to immediately develop a positive tone. The answer he gives is structured (with a good ending summation) and draws from past project work while establishing relevancy and linkages to consulting. The candidate illustrates skills in leadership, client relations, working in teams, thinking creatively, being action oriented, and managing the all-important 80/20 rule—each important traits of a successful consultant. Depending on time allotment, this candidate could have even gone into more detail in describing his work at Merrill.

Candidate: As I think about improvement opportunities, a couple things come to mind. Consultants convey many of their research, findings, and recommendations in slide presentations. As such, this is a critical art to master. I haven't had a lot of experience in this and will likely have room to improve the packaging of my work. I would address this by writing slides, soliciting feedback, and looking over past presentations that had real client impact. Additionally, my experience to date has had me rolling up my sleeves and doing the execution myself. While I know consultants often get involved in implementation, it is very important to educate the client along the way so they are self-sufficient in the long run. This education mode is something I will improve on over time, as well.

The candidate presents a thoughtful answer that points to fairly common issues among new consultants and that doesn't raise any serious concerns. Both issues are addressable with time. More importantly, the candidate impressively talks to how he would go about addressing the improvement opportunities. Again, showing his orientation for action. Finally, both points further illustrate his understanding of consulting, which is far favorable to a candidate who does not know what he or she is getting into.

Case 14

I see that you worked at a dot com for a year, before moving to a large bank for two years. What do you see as the pros and cons for you of working in a large organization versus a small organization? What would you bring to consulting from your experiences in two very different working environments?

Whether the job history of an MBA or the internship per academic history of an undergrad, the underlying takeaway is the same. The interviewer is probing linkages and consistency throughout the resume, and how the mix of activities has yielded an interest in consulting. Most interviewers are more interested in the person and their story (e.g., motivations, past decisions, professional interests) when conducting resume interviews than in discussing specific bullet points (which they will have already read and evaluated on their own). They are carefully searching to answer not only whether you are right for consulting, but whether consulting is right for you. It is important to be ready to speak to any seemingly inconsistent steps along the chronology of your resume; whether you go from banking to a dot com or banking to the Peace Corps.

Bad Answer

Candidate: Large organizations are too structured. Things take a long time to get accomplished and strategic decisions get stuck in bureaucratic bottlenecks. They also have so many divisions, groups, and layers of decision making, that communication is always suboptimal. Small companies require employees to do everything from fixing the copy machine to ordering supplies to drawing up a strategic plan and executing it. Plus, unless you are among the top brass, you will not reap the rewards if they begin to rocket into financial success. Pros? I would say job security is a pro at a large company and small companies offer employees more access to senior management. My experiences in both environments would make me a good consultant because I have a first-hand sense of these pros and cons.

Pros are a good place to start, rather than cons. But this is the least of the candidate's concerns. He clearly had some bad experiences and is displaying a bitter attitude. His assertions are harsh generalizations about both environments, which may make the interviewer question his interest in the consulting firm itself. The main problem with this answer is it is more accusatory than getting to the pros and cons as they specifically apply to the kind of person the candidate is. Finally, the candidate gave a non-answer for the last part of the question.

Good Answer

Candidate: Recognizing that all organizations are different, I will speak to what I observed in my experiences. I had a very valuable experience at the dot com, both in good times and bad. Entrepreneurship was a pervasive attitude in the company and each individual was encouraged to run with his ideas. This was a good fit for me, as it generated passion and a sense of ownership that made the mission to build something from nothing quite a motivating adventure. I found it a challenge, however, to grow under extreme uncertainty and lack of financial resources. This was a distraction at first and ultimately led to our demise.

Good start. The candidate begins by avoiding generalizations, disclaiming that all organizations are different—Microsoft would not consider itself a typical large company, for example. He also recognizes the positive value of good and bad experiences to a person's development. He clearly highlights the motivating effect on him of an entrepreneurial environment, and then explains, without appearing negative, the challenges of uncertainty and access to capital.

Candidate: As I considered career options, I wanted to maintain the entrepreneurial atmosphere, but in a more structured environment where there was access to capital and a strong support network to feed growth. I found a small incubator group in a large bank and accepted a position where I could leverage my dot com experience in helping grow small companies in our portfolio, while helping to build the group from the ground up. It really was the best of both worlds for me at first. Being a large organization, there were many business groups with different agendas and priorities that were not effectively communicated. Ultimately the incubator was not absorbed effectively into the organization because of perceived conflicts of interest and a general lack of appetite for a changed business model.

The candidate draws a clear linkage of moving from the dot com to the large bank. He also shows his creativity in finding a startup-like opportunity under the umbrella of a large, resource-rich organization. He goes on to explain the difficulty the company had with accepting change and ironing out real or perceived conflicts of interest across different groups.

Candidate: My experiences taught me a lot. They taught me that I like working on small teams with a clean slate from which to creatively build an optimal path forward. I also found that despite what happened to the incubator group, I enjoyed the feeling of being supported by a larger organization with sufficient resources. Working on a project-by-project basis in small teams within a large consulting firm will meet my interests well. My experiences afford me the ability to work well in small teams and address many different problem types. Additionally, I would bring a strong desire for helping ensure that communication lines are open and efficient across consulting teams and industry practices within the firm, to leverage resources and avoid clashes in strategic directions. Finally, having worked in large and small environments, I would be able to interact effectively with various sizes of client organizations.

The candidate finishes strongly by explaining what he got from his experiences and why it is driving his interest in consulting. He goes on to highlight what of his past experiences he brings to consulting, thus positioning his situation in a unique, value-added way.

Case 15

I see you led a cross-functional merger integration team at General Electric. What is your leadership style?

This is a common yet highly important resume question. The interviewer is trying to gauge how you will structure and lead team-based projects (or modules within a project), how you will develop and motivate others around you (peers, managers, and subordinates alike), and how you will interact with client employees. At the same time, the interviewer is indirectly seeking some description of the specific merger project listed on the resume.

Bad Answer

Candidate: I like to avoid the team dynamic of having too many people providing too many ideas and solutions. I thus like to make it clear that I am leading the project and that while open to suggestions, I will make the final decisions on how we attack a problem. I have found that when people are left to their own devices, projects can skew out of focus and become overwhelming to control. I hold people accountable for their actions and find that to be very motivating.

This candidate is a bit aggressive in his leadership style. He does not demonstrate a strong sense of teamwork. He also does not seem to understand that such leadership tactics used in his previous organization may not work well in a consulting environment. Consulting teams consist of several highly motivated, self-starting, and intelligent people who typically function most effectively under a more collaborative style of leadership. It is important to frame your experiences and style in the context of the position for which you are being evaluated. This candidate also failed to speak about his experience leading the merger team.

Good Answer

Candidate: I first try to learn a little about my teammates. This was critical in leading the cross-functional team at GE, as learning the strengths and experiences of team members from marketing, R&D, IT, sales, and customer support, gave me a comprehensive picture of what needed to be done. This allowed me to carefully structure a work plan with logically assigned roles and under reasonable timeframes. I also find that when a team is part of the plan creation process, they will be more motivated in executing against it.

Good beginning. The candidate seems to be illustrating his style by going down a chronological path of leading a project team. He also brings his experience directly into his answer, while explaining the benefits of his technique. Overall, this candidate clearly conveys that he is a team player.

After putting the plan together, I like to present it to the team for discussion and to clarify primary objectives and action items. I then follow up with team members individually to gauge what they are looking to get out of the project, if they are happy with their role, and if they are clear on deliverables and timeframes. I then let them go at it, without micromanaging their activity. Frequent updates with the team are critical, as I strive to maintain open lines of communication to facilitate knowledge sharing and establish a collaborative team dynamic. In my experience at GE, this allowed me to redirect when necessary and ensured that we were all on the same page. As the project progresses and deliverables start to come in from team members, I like to offer feedback and mentorship so they are able to develop their skill sets in real time. Having said all that, I believe it is important to have some fun along the way. At GE, we would try to have a team event weekly, such as eating at a nice restaurant, playing volleyball, or going to a show together.

The candidate clearly articulated his collaborative style that believes in open communication, encouragement, and feedback. He also made it clear that he has a very tactical style (e.g., plans, deliverables, stated objectives, roles). He has highlighted parts of his style most relevant to the tactical, team-oriented nature of consulting. Plus he expressed the importance of fun, a necessity if one is to enjoy the intense demands of consulting.

WETFEET'S INSIDER GUIDE SERIES

JOB SEARCH GUIDES

Getting Your Ideal Internship

Job Hunting A to Z: Landing the Job You Want

Killer Consulting Resumes!

Killer Investment Banking Resumes!

Killer Cover Letters & Resumes!

Negotiating Your Salary & Perks

Networking Works!

INTERVIEW GUIDES

Ace Your Case: Consulting Interviews

Ace Your Case II: 15 More Consulting Cases

Ace Your Case III: Practice Makes Perfect

Ace Your Case IV: The Latest & Greatest

Ace Your Case V: Return to the Case Interview

Ace Your Interview!

Beat the Street: Investment Banking Interviews

Beat the Street II: I-Banking Interview Practice Guide

CAREER & INDUSTRY GUIDES

Careers in Accounting

Careers in Advertising & Public Relations

Careers in Asset Management & Retail Brokerage

Careers in Biotech & Pharmaceuticals

Careers in Brand Management

Careers in Consumer Products

Careers in Entertainment & Sports

Careers in Human Resources

Careers in Information Technology

Careers in Investment Banking

Careers in Management Consulting

Careers in Manufacturing

Careers in Marketing & Market Research

Careers in Nonprofits & Government Agencies

Careers in Real Estate

Careers in Supply Chain Management

Careers in Venture Capital

Consulting for PhDs, Doctors & Lawyers

Industries & Careers for MBAs

Industries & Careers for Undergrads

COMPANY GUIDES

Accenture

Bain & Company

Boston Consulting Group

Booz Allen Hamilton

Citigroup's Corporate & Investment Bank

Credit Suisse First Boston

Deloitte Consulting

Goldman Sachs Group

J.P. Morgan Chase & Company

Lehman Brothers

McKinsey & Company

Merrill Lynch

Morgan Stanley

25 Top Consulting Firms

Top 20 Biotechnology & Pharmaceuticals Firms

Top 25 Financial Services Firms